LIVE
FOR WHAT
OUTLIVES
YOU

Bill McKenzie
Founder of Pine Cove Christian Camps

Produced with the assistance of Fluency Organization, Inc. in Tyler, Texas. Design and layout by DK Designs Group. Cover by Inkwell Creative. Cover photo by Josiah White.

Printed in the United States of America.

"Bill McKenzie's book is an enjoyable read, especially for those who have experienced a Pine Cove conference. But it is much more than that. It is a call to all of us to, as the title suggests, 'Live for What Outlives You.' I highly recommend it for everyone, whether you have attended a Pine Cove conference or not."

Jerry Bridges
Author of *Pursuit of Holiness* and
staff member with The Navigators

"God can easily do His mighty works in a vacuum, but usually He lays a vision on someone whose faithfulness and persistence ultimately become the platform for God's majesty. Many of these 'mighty works' are decades upon decades in the making. Pine Cove is a great example of this. God needed someone to say 'Yes' to Him a long time ago and maintain a vision for what could be through all of the circumstances that would incline more timid souls to give up. *Live for What Outlives You* is that man's story . . . and *His* story."

Dr. Tim Kimmel
Author of *Grace Based Parenting* and
Grace Filled Marriage

"Bill McKenzie is an amazing man with an amazing story. His life as an aeronautical engineer and a devoted follower of Jesus Christ finds its nexus in the vision and values of Pine Cove. He is a man of faith who has removed the word 'impossible' from his personal dictionary. His story of passion and persistence for the birth and growth of Pine Cove is a story that will bless anyone who is on a journey of faith. As his pastor and friend, I highly recommend *Live for What Outlives You*."

Dr. David O. Dykes
Senior Pastor, Green Acres Baptist
Church, Tyler, Texas
Author of *No, That's Not in the Bible*
and *Revelation: God's Final Word*

"Having known Bill McKenzie and his family for over 58 years, I have followed his journey with the Lord and have personally experienced the ministry of Pine Cove. The success of Pine Cove from a human standpoint is the vision of one man who was willing to trust God in the face of seeming impossibilities. Bill's personal experiences add color to the book and make for interesting reading. Probably the true story of Pine Cove is hidden beneath the written words in the book: God honors those who willingly give Him the glory for all that is accomplished. "

> Dr. Wendell Johnston
> Former Pastor, McKinney Memorial
> Bible Church,
> Fort Worth, Texas

"This is a story about God showing up and showing off! Bill McKenzie is a man of faith, vision and action. This is a must-read book for any person who wants to live a life that truly does outlive you. This book will challenge you to believe God for too much, rather than too little."

> Dr. Dennis Rainey
> President, FamilyLife

"Bill McKenzie's autobiography strikes several important chords in my life, and I dare say it will do the same for future readers. God prepared a special plan of commitment to Christ Jesus and unique service to His Kingdom on earth for Bill. And Bill responded! I strongly recommend you read this moving encounter between a remarkable and gifted businessman, husband, father, sports nut and his God."

> Jerry Kindall
> Retired Major League Baseball
> player and former Baseball Coach at
> the University of Arizona

To my mother, Margaret Thorburn McKenzie, and my father, Alexander Winfred McKenzie. And to Sharon Harris McKenzie, my wife of 58 years. All have shaped and supported my life for many years.

I am a wealthy man. I am a manager of what God owns.

My time

My gifts

My vision

My discernment

My insight

My heritage

My energy

My maturity

My legacy

God owns it all.

DEUTERONOMY 8:11-18

Table of Contents

Foreword

I REMEMBER THAT DAY AS IF IT WERE YESTERDAY. I was on my way to a singles retreat at a Christian camp. I was a relatively new follower of Christ—really struggling as I straddled my old life with the reality of being a new creation in Christ and having a new life.

As I pulled into the camp, a peace fell over me. As I drove through the tree-lined entrance, something happened. That night the person leading the worship time led us in a song where one of the lines was, "With one hand reach out to Jesus, and with another, bring a friend." That is exactly what someone did for me. I wept. I would never be the same. Little did I know this was the beginning of a journey that would encompass over half of my life.

In 1987 with two young kids in tow, Lynelle and I went to Pine Cove for Family Camp. Another young couple, Doug and Jill Chesnut, invited us. Jill was the daughter of Bill and Sharon McKenzie. It was during this week that I first met Bill. He was passionate about Pine Cove, passionate about families and passionate about Jesus. He invited our entire group in as if we were family. I remember meeting Sharon and thinking that Bill was able to do what he was doing because she was willing to love him through thick and thin.

This began a journey in which I would move from camper, to Advisory Board Member, to Board Member and eventually to CEO of Pine Cove.

As a member of the Board of Directors, I began to see something about Pine Cove that I did not fully understand. It was a place where life change and life transformation happens. Two years into my term, Dan Bolin, the beloved Executive Director of Pine Cove, stepped down. For some crazy reason, the Board thought I ought to be on the search committee. Bill was the head of the search committee, and we pursued a traditional approach to finding a new leader. At one of the search committee meetings (while I was out of town), Bill shared the idea of hiring a businessperson with ministry passion instead of a ministry person with business experience. The search committee agreed, and that put Pine Cove on a new trajectory.

I vividly remember the day that Bill and I discussed my becoming a candidate for the job. As I shared with Bill what I was thinking, he responded with tears in his eyes, "I have been thinking about you all along. I just didn't think you would quit your job." Even though I assured him that I just wanted to be a candidate, I think he and I both knew what God had in store.

Later that week Bill and I drove around in his old 4-wheel drive SUV, and he shared his dreams of what Pine Cove could become. All I had to do was take notes and pay close attention. Bill lived and breathed Pine Cove. He mentored me, coached me and cared for me—in some ways better than my own dad could. Bill got me and I got him.

I have watched Bill win and lose, rejoice and have pain and endure the longsuffering road of success and failure—trusting Jesus every step of the way. Bill is living proof that what he was involved in will outlive him. Literally, heaven will be populated by tens of thousands of people who made a profession of faith in Jesus at Pine Cove. God used Bill in a profound way to shape the future of over a million campers in the nearly 50 years Pine Cove has been a ministry.

His fingerprints are on the ministry and on thousands of campers who have stepped onto the holy ground known as Pine Cove. He has had a faithful commitment to endure where many a man would have given up along the way.

Enjoy this book. I am confident this story will bless you. Live in such a way that your impact will outlive you . . . just as Bill has.

Mario Zandstra
Former CEO of Pine Cove
(1998 to January 2015)

Acknowledgments

Without Mary Ann Lackland and her company Fluency Organization, Inc., this book would not exist. Mary Ann has skillfully drawn out of me details of my life, then creatively put them into stories that make you want to turn the page. My wife Sharon's tenacious proofreading helped make an accurate manuscript.

Special thanks also to the Staff and Board of Pine Cove Christian Camps that believed this book would have a message before they saw it. Without their love and dedication to serve the Body of Christ, there would not be a book worth writing.

LIVE FOR WHAT OutLIVES You

Introduction

Sharon and I have been on the grounds at Pine Cove quite a bit in recent years, either attending youth camp closing celebrations or hearing various speakers at family camps. As we start to walk out of the room, people often come up to us and exclaim, "How on earth did Pine Cove get started? What motivated you?" People are curious how this ministry got started. One of the reasons I decided to write this book was in answer to those types of questions.

Second, I wanted to write this book while my memory is still strong. I wanted to acknowledge how many others had helped along the way. It all adds up to a line from the old hymn by Fanny Crosby, "To God be the glory, great things He has done."

The third reason I wanted to write this book has to do with my family. I want our children, grandchildren, their children and so on to know how good God was to provide my Christian heritage. I want to challenge them to not slide through life enamored with the things of earth during their short while here. My hope is that they will catch the real, eternal "disease" of being in love with the Lord Jesus Christ.

In this book I weave together stories from my personal life along with generations of Christian heritage that prepared me in my early thirties to conceptualize both a business and a ministry plan with the potential to be what Pine Cove is today. It is my fervent hope and prayer that this book will challenge young and old alike about their dreams and God-given vision in such a way that they decide to obey God and step out in faith. I am a guy who barely made it through school. Although I aspired to be an athlete, I was not one. Nor did I come home from college to inherit a family business! I did not know any better than to believe God. He did not look for my ability; all He needed was my availability.

"Only one life, 'twill soon be past. Only what's done for Christ will last."
– C.T. Studd

LIVE FOR WHAT OutLIVES YOU

LIVE
FOR WHAT
OUTLIVES
YOU

CHAPTER 1

A Showplace for God's Glory

"I am going to bless this land with a showplace for My glory."

THE SOUND OF LEAVES CRUNCHING ON THE FOREST FLOOR INTERRUPTED MY THOUGHTS AS I MADE MY WAY TO INSPECT A SMALL WOOD AND METAL BRIDGE A FRIEND OF MINE HAD BUILT FOR ME ACROSS A SHALLOW CREEK ON OUR FAMILY PROPERTY. The tree-filled forest was 78 acres of land perfectly situated along the shore of a small East Texas lake outside Tyler, Texas. It had belonged to my family since I was a young boy. With the trained eye of an engineer, I immediately began analyzing the sturdiness of this little addition to our property as I took a few steps across the bridge. It seemed solid underneath my feet and I quietly felt a sense of pride that we'd been able to put it together using leftover bar-joists from a construction job at a local shopping center. As a child I'd seen my father patiently pull out nails with a hammer from an old piece of wood and straighten them so they could be used again. So, the idea of being resourceful

Original family cabin

was not lost on me.

All morning I had been consumed with thoughts about a major decision that my family and I had faced for some time now. I wasn't quite sure what to do, and I had not yet heard a definitive answer from God. I had, however, earnestly prayed about it as much as a young man could pray about something that could potentially affect his entire family's future.

Standing on the bridge, I took a slow look around at my family's sanctuary for over two decades. Our Hyannis Port, we had called it, nicknaming it after the famous Kennedy family compound that had captivated the American public in the 1960s Camelot era. I thought of all the times Dad and I had fished in the nearby lake. I wasn't much of one for fishing, but I enjoyed paddling him around so he could cast a line into those placid waters after work. I recalled the four of us, including my mother, Margaret, and older brother, Robert, sitting down at a little table we had set up in the cabin for a freshly-caught fish dinner. There was no running water in those days. Before Dad had eventually talked the power company into running a line over to our place, we would read in the evenings by candlelight from oil lamps. My cousins, aunts and uncles also came to visit on

1323 Mockingbird Lane

long weekends in the lazy days of summer. It was fun to pretend we were pioneers out in the Wild West, catching rainwater that fell on the rooftop into a barrel, which we used for cleaning. We also carried water from home in Tyler.

It wasn't much, this small place in the woods, but it was ours. Yet, for how much longer would it be just ours? I wasn't sure. Was there something more we were supposed to do with our little haven? I couldn't escape that nagging thought. Some would say that Dad had lucked into owning this property—a simple matter of being in the right place at the right time. But we knew better. God was in it all along.

My dad, Alex McKenzie, had worked his way up from teller to senior trust officer at Tyler State Bank over many years. One day he met with a man who would change the course of our family's lives. The man was a car dealer who walked into his office one Tuesday and announced, "Alex, I've got to sell that piece of lake property by Friday this week." Dad knew the property well, since he had leased the land to graze some cows long before the lake was built. The man continued, "Do you know anyone who might want to buy it? I'll let it go for $5000."

There wasn't much discretionary cash in 1944. America was in the final stages of the fight against a battle-weary Germany and a beleaguered Japan in World War II. Life at home in America during the war meant daily sacrifice and rationing of goods, but people rarely complained. They knew those serving overseas were making the much greater sacrifice.

Many people in the East Texas community, especially in Tyler, had profited from a local lucrative oil boom around that time and had been able to build beautiful homes. However, Mother and Dad were always quick to let us know we did not come from money, and they raised us to value a dollar. Mother and Dad had met in the small Texas town of Kerrville, where I was born in 1930 at the start of the Great Depression. We lived in San Antonio for a time where Dad had started a small refrigeration business. When it failed, he moved us to Tyler to start over in an entry-level position at Tyler State Bank. I spent most of my childhood growing up at 1323 Mockingbird Lane, drinking milk from our own cows and eating eggs from our chickens and eating butter Mother made herself.

Five thousand dollars was a lot of money—too much money for Dad to come up with on his own and with such short notice. He then approached a couple of other business partners about the opportunity, and by Friday afternoon we were part owners of 78 acres and a primitive cabin with no running water and no electricity.

Mother had initially been afraid of looking auspicious. However, over time she seemed to warm to the idea of owning this property for the McKenzie family. Dad toyed with the idea of putting it back on the market for $20,000 (which was closer to its real value), but Mother's prayerful intuition led her to believe God had other plans. I later heard her one night talking with Dad about the potential of buying out the other property owners some day when we could afford it. That way, she explained, the property would belong solely to our family and rule out any possibility of being sold in the future. No one at the time understood the importance of this decision, but it was definitely

LIVE FOR WHAT OutLIVES You

providential. She had a special feeling about this land. As all of us men in the McKenzie family had learned from experience to do, Dad agreed with Mother's advice and soon bought out the other partners.

I was fourteen when Dad first bought the property in 1944. It was about this same time that my childhood fascination with airplanes began to peak. As a young boy, I had built model airplanes, as most young boys do at one time or another. However, I was unusually motivated because we were at war. In fact, the War Department had asked young boys like me to build models of bombers and fighter craft to educate American soldiers on how to distinguish enemy planes from American planes. I worked from restricted plans of Japanese, German and Allied planes supplied by Camp Fannin, a local U.S. Army training center in Tyler.

I also worked a paper route for the *Tyler Morning Telegraph* and saved all my money so I could take my first ride in an airplane out at Stewart Field. I did not tell Mother about my secret mission, as I had learned it was sometimes better to ask for her forgiveness rather than for her permission! Those 30 minutes up in the air

Building model airplanes

were the best two dollars I'd ever spent. It was a small training plane, nothing fancy. It was also very loud and bumpy as it banged down the dirt runway before launching into the sky. We banked toward downtown Tyler, and as I took in the views from several thousand feet high, I knew I was hooked.

I made it my goal to work hard and become "Tyler's youngest

private pilot." I figured if I could get my pilot's license at seventeen, I could set that record. Over the next two years, I spent nearly every waking moment thinking about planes. One day I went to Tyler Pounds Field airport and asked if there were any jobs. They hired me to pull the trainer planes out of the hangar in the morning and tie them down. If any were dirty, I would wash them until they sparkled. I never received any pay—just applied my earnings toward flying lessons, which I began at sixteen. I also drove an old International Harvester truck the guys at the Coats McCain Lumber Company called Granny. I would grind that lowest gear hard and get her going down the road to make my deliveries, leaving behind a cloud of black smoke and a group of guys laughing in the yard.

The day I soloed a J-3 Piper Cub on runway 4 at Tyler Pounds Field was one of the best days of my young life. I then started preparing for my cross-country solo flight, the last step in the process of securing my private pilot's license. All of my training thus far had been in the Piper Cub at Pounds Field, but with my seventeenth birthday drawing near and my piggy bank running low, I got creative. I went across town to Stewart Field where the plane rental was a little cheaper to make my solo cross-country flight. Little did I know that decision, motivated by my youthful pride of wanting to set the record, would prove costly.

On the morning of my departure, I walked around the Luscombe aircraft with side-by-side seating, conducting a pre-flight inspection as I had done dozens of times before. I checked to see that the tires had plenty of air and that the oil and fuel levels were satisfactory. I moved the control surfaces on the trailing edge of the wings to see that they were free and clear. However, this was a different plane than the one I was used to flying, so I took some extra time to familiarize myself with it. I put my navigation maps in the co-pilot's seat and waved one final time to my parents. Then I started taxiing down the runway for the first leg of my solo flight to Waco, about 200 miles southwest. The plan was to fly from Tyler south to Waco, then head up to Dallas and back east to Tyler. Everything went smoothly as I climbed to my pre-selected altitude. As I leveled off, I was already thinking to myself, "This shouldn't be too hard."

However, I saw the unmistakably dark clouds of a rainstorm ahead. I knew I had to stay clear of clouds, so I veered left, intending to go around the storm and then get back on course. However, it took me longer to circumvent the storm than I intended. I soon realized I was hopelessly lost. This was before the time of electronic navigation aids and radar. The main way pilots navigated was by a method called dead reckoning. It was an imprecise navigational method that identified your current position based upon a known previous position. But since I was lost, even dead reckoning was useless.

Fighting the controls with one hand, I pulled a map into my lap with the other and wrestled to unfold it. I then lowered the nose to buzz a water tower ahead of me in an effort to read the town's name off of it. The name was not familiar. I flew over several more small towns, buzzing water towers but not recognizing any names. I prayed for God to help me. I was in a serious dilemma and I wasn't sure which way to go.

I had been lost one other time with another pilot, and I recalled how he had landed in a pasture where he talked to the farmer, got his bearings and resumed our flight. In my case, I then spotted a wide-open pasture and proceeded to make a perfect landing. I got out of the plane and walked over to the barn where a surprised farmer stood holding a bucket of feed.

"Good morning!" I said, trying my best to appear as if seeing a teenager pop out of a small aircraft by himself in 1947 was commonplace.

"Son, you okay?" he asked and slowly set the bucket down, wiping his gnarled hands on his overalls before taking my outstretched hand in a handshake.

I explained my predicament and asked which direction was Buffalo, one of the checkpoints along my route to Waco. He pointed a dirt-covered finger west. "Thataway, about 30 miles," he said dryly, still eyeing me with disbelief.

My first and only crash

I thanked him and cheerily made my way back to the plane, even though my heart was pounding because of the trouble I'd found myself in. By this time his wife had joined his side, with a few small children wrapped around her legs. They all stood speechless, staring as I turned the plane around in their pasture to take off again.

I slowly advanced the throttle to full power and soon the Luscombe was bouncing along down the field. Before I reached lift off speed, I heard a loud bang. I assumed it was the right landing gear hitting a ditch on the unlevel ground. I tried to stop, but I had gathered so much speed at that point that I crossed a road, took out a pair of barbed wire fences and bounced over two ditches. Through the windshield, I next saw a barn quickly approaching. I stood on the brake pedals hoping to stop short of it, but the momentum of the plane caused it to slam into the barn, nose first.

In the sudden silence, I was praying and confessing my foolishness in attempting something I clearly was not prepared to do. Then I made sure that I was not injured, realizing Mother would have been so upset at me if I'd been hurt. I was fine, as far as I could tell, but I couldn't say the same about the airplane. Trembling with adrenaline, I slowly climbed out of the cockpit door. I walked on shaky legs over to my

LIVE FOR WHAT OutLIVES YOU

Bridge at Pine Cove

farmer friend and sheepishly asked if I could use his phone to call Dad. Later that afternoon the owner of the plane flew down to meet me and take me back home to my parents. As it turned out, I was only four miles from an airport when I landed in the pasture! Insurance would cover the expense, but it would be some time before the damage to my wounded pride healed. Even so, I did end up getting my private pilot's license two weeks after my seventeenth birthday on July 15, 1947.

Now, 20 years later in 1967, I found myself lost at a crossroads again—this time trying to determine God's will for my future. I wasn't sure which way to go and like that teenager in the pilot's seat, I had prayed for God to help me see my way clear to make a decision and act quickly.

So much time had passed since those early days of my youth, I thought, as I took a few more steps across the bar joist bridge. I had since gone to college, graduated, gotten married and had been living in Fort Worth working as an aeronautical engineer. I was in my mid-thirties with a family to think of and a potentially lucrative career ahead of me. So, why was I considering making a 180-degree turn in the direction of a Christian camping ministry of all things? Many events had transpired in the past few years in relation to this property, especially in the previous 18 months. It was hard to discern for certain what God wanted to do next. What was the future of this place? Was there something I wasn't yet seeing?

I had just made it to the midpoint of the bridge when I "heard" a voice. I spun around, expecting to greet Don Hill, my friend in the construction business who had built the bridge. But I was alone, and the only sound was the distant, familiar caw of a black crow.

What occurred next was the most vivid experience that has ever happened to me. It wasn't an audible voice I'd heard—it was much louder than that. "Bill, I am going to bless this land with a showplace for My glory," the voice seemed to say. At the time, I felt in my heart that it was God speaking some sort of undeniable revelation. Like Moses, this was my burning bush moment, and I did not need to hear Him repeat it. I quickened my steps back to my car. I had two phone calls to make.

CHAPTER 2

Straddling the Fence

"I was tired of fighting against God's plan for me. I was ready to yield to Him."

"Thorburn McKenzie, just what do you think you are doing?"

Mother stood at the door of my room. I was in high school, packing a bag to head to Fun Forest pool in Tyler with some friends from school. I had my swim trunks on and carried a towel under my arm.

"Mother . . . " I winced as I explained that I was just going to meet some of the guys at the pool, but I already knew what concerned her. Mother had always insisted I wear a top with my swimsuit. I was embarrassed because no other guy wore a top to the swimming pool, but despite my resentment, I obeyed her. She was raised in a conservative home herself, with her father studying for the pastorate in Scotland. William Thorburn, my grandfather and namesake, had studied theology in Scotland before crossing the Atlantic Ocean to continue his studies in theology in Clarksville, Tennessee, in 1892, where he met my grandmother Emma.

A widow from the time Grandfather Thorburn died of tuberculosis in his early forties, my grandmother lived with us during different periods of my childhood and had a great spiritual influence on me. Like her mother, my mother was also a great

student of Scripture and very familiar with theological issues. She and Dad would later be part of the founding meeting of the Presbyterian Church in America (PCA) in Alabama in 1973 that sought to preserve the cardinal truths of the Word of God. They were also founding members of Fifth Street Presbyterian Church PCA in Tyler.

I was saved when I was seven years old at a child evangelism class my mother taught. Christ was the center of my family's life, due to the godly heritage I inherited from my mother's side. Yet, as a teen, I had one foot in the world, working hard to maintain my popularity and dating the head cheerleader—and one foot in the faith. I knew the Bible because of my upbringing and had all the right answers. I was a Christian, but truth be told, I wasn't sure that I wanted Christ to be at the head of my life if it meant I could never have any fun.

Top: Margaret McKenzie
Bottom: Alex McKenzie

I was a typical teenager and had grown resistant to my parents' faith, although outwardly I continued going through the motions. I wasn't rebellious, and my brother and I were both involved in the local Young Life club. I just didn't like standing out from my peers because of the uncomfortable and confining conservatism that pervaded our home. Mother did not even allow me to go to dances or movies, although I did sneak off a time or two to meet some girls and guys at the Tyler Theater downtown. I always wanted to see the latest romantic film from Cary Grant, Ingrid Bergman or Donna Reed. Although these black-and-white goldies from the forties were mild compared to today, Mother was very afraid of Hollywood tempting her boys.

I remember one time the school assigned my cheerleader girlfriend a date to go to the prom, since I could not take her to the dance at Tyler High School. I can still remember the sick feeling I had knowing I had to let my own girlfriend go with another boy. Even my name made me different from my peers—Thorburn (which Mother hung on me since she and her two sisters had no chance of passing on the family surname).

I was the laughing stock at the pool with my cover-up and was sometimes ridiculed at school for being a religious stick-in-the-mud. However, the other kids had no idea how much I was struggling. I had played neighborhood sports all my life, but I was hardly the athlete I'd always dreamed of becoming. I was rounding

Top: Emma Thorburn
Bottom: Meet a Tyler lion

the bases at Wrigley Field in my imagination, sitting by the old Emerson radio in our living room, listening to the play-by-play from the announcer. In reality I was second string at best. I also wanted

Young Life Board, Dad standing on far right

to wake up one day and be popular and free of religious constraints, but my life wasn't turning out to be anything like I'd planned.

When I was on the high school football team, they called me "Little Hightower" and the "understudy" for the first string center, Dick Hightower. I played with the two sons of Mr. Wood Brookshire, the founder of a successful grocery company he started in East Texas called Brookshire's. He used to come by our practices and talk to the boys on the sideline with some of the other dads. One day one of the dads jokingly told us to smash each other's faces in the mud. He wasn't being mean—he just wanted to see how we would react to adversity in an effort to toughen us. As much as we don't like it, we all need hard times to build perseverance and learn to rally back from difficulty. God was using these circumstances to toughen me. Like that dad, He was doing it because He loved me. But I didn't much like it.

Dad served on the national board of Young Life as the treasurer, starting when I was twelve until I was in my late twenties. In fact, Jim Rayburn, the founder of Young Life, visited our Tyler Young Life Club in 1942 and my parents helped host him. Jim mentions my parents by name in his published diary.[1] Dad was

[1] *Jim Rayburn's Diaries*, Whitecaps Media, 2008.

LIVE FOR WHAT OUT**LIVES** YOU

on the board, but I was on the fence spiritually speaking. It wouldn't be until I was in college that I decided once and for all to surrender my entire life to Christ. Not surprisingly it was the influence of Young Life that helped me settle the issue. A man named George Sheffer, the second leader of the original Young Life Club in Tyler, had often lovingly prodded me as a high school student to truly embrace my faith. And it was Jim Rayburn who helped me understand what it meant to serve Christ the summer I volunteered at Star Ranch in Colorado before my senior year in college. Star Ranch was the premier Young life camp for teens. It served as a model for other camps.

I was working as a wrangler that summer, drawing on my experience with the horses we'd had in the pasture behind our home on Mockingbird Lane in Tyler. Each week Jim would deliver a powerful 20-minute "sermon" to campers about the Gospel. He always said that if a speaker couldn't "get it done" with high school kids in 20 minutes or less, he shouldn't even try. I was mesmerized by the way Jim held their attention and kept them on the edge of their seats the entire time he spoke. I also saw firsthand how presenting the truth of the Gospel in a camp setting made it easier for kids to accept the message and respond to it.

"It's okay if you've never ridden a horse," Jim would jokingly tell the kids on the first day they came to see me at the barn. "Mac's got horses that have never been ridden." I was going by Mac now, a change I'd made when I was living on my own in college. Not only was I going by a different name, I was at a new place in my faith. Living at a Christian camp for an entire summer, I had developed an entirely new perspective on Christianity. I saw men and women who were free to live out a dynamic, personal relationship with Christ, not just keep rules. I also became very involved volunteering in Young Life, first when I was at Spartan College in Tulsa, Oklahoma, and then when I transferred to Oklahoma University in Norman.

Several other things happened that summer at Star Ranch and in college that God would use to further get my attention. During a week of camp at Star Ranch, one of our campers became ill. She was a girl from Tyler and actually ended up in the hospital in Colorado Springs. Knowing I was from Tyler, an older counselor named Marjorie came to the corral and suggested I accompany her to the hospital to visit the young camper. I wasn't necessarily keen on this idea, as I didn't really know what I could do to cheer up a young girl. Years later that sick camper would recall the details specifically and recount how I sat silently in the corner in boots and jeans, my hat pulled down over my brow. I don't remember much about the visit, and I had no way of knowing that this first encounter would someday alter my life forever.

Something else began taking place in the form of a series of divine encounters that would continue my entire life. For the second time God allowed me to cross paths with people whom He would use mightily in the Kingdom (the first being Jim Rayburn). I remember seeing my good friend, Jerry, at Oklahoma University soon after I transferred there. We had grown up together in Tyler and even played football on the same team in high school. One day on the Oklahoma University campus I invited him to a Bible study hosted by a Christian organization called The Navigators. Jerry had grown up in a Baptist church but didn't know about The Navigators, an international parachurch ministry for discipleship that started in 1933. I was familiar with them because of my background in Young Life, which used The Navigators' follow-up system of Scripture verses on cards and Bible studies.

After Jerry attended his first Navigators Bible study, he soon jumped in and began attending much more than I did! Jerry Bridges was a dedicated Christian from a strong family of faith and continued serving with The Navigators long after graduating from OU, eventually becoming the Vice President! My second daughter Allison once wrote me from college about how much she was enjoying a book on discipleship, *The Pursuit of Holiness*. "It's written by a man named

Jerry Bridges from Tyler. Do you know him?" she asked one day.

"I grew up with him," I told her, fondly recalling how far the Lord had brought both of us. Our Tyler High School class of 1947 had a reunion every five years. There were usually around 150 people in attendance, including spouses. I was asked to chair the 50th reunion and bring a little seriousness to the occasion. I asked Jerry to give a talk on how to finish strong in life. I still remember one of the points he shared that night. Jerry said, "Relationships are more important than accomplishments." Since I have always been an accomplishments-oriented person, this truth hit me hard.

From the time we were young men, Jerry had always seemed to know the path God chose for him. It would be many years before I would realize exactly what God had called me to do. I took classes in the summer of 1951 in Norman as an upperclassman. About 900 missionaries with Wycliffe Bible Translators were also on campus that summer attending the Institute of Linguistics. I was familiar with Wycliffe and their desire to make God's Word available in every language in the world. The young men and women volunteering with Wycliffe were only a little older than I was, and they had a vibrant faith.

Riding horses in Tyler

One night I ran into a young man named Jim who was determined that I come with him to worship with the students from Wycliffe. He was a compact, muscular guy and I was almost afraid to say no to him! Walking to the outdoor amphitheater that muggy June night, Jim told me of his plans to serve God as a missionary. Just a few years later, I would open my newspaper to discover the tragic news that this same young man, Jim Elliot, and four other missionaries in the jungles of Ecuador had been martyred while sharing the Gospel. I recalled his passion for the Lord, standing next to him that night as he and hundreds of young people sang out at the top of their lungs a cappella, "O for a Thousand Tongues to Sing." I knew my life would never be the same after that night.

In fact I had met another friend named Jerry Elder during the summer I worked at Star Ranch. Jerry had decided to leave Young Life to also serve in South America with Wycliffe. He was the state Young Life leader for Oklahoma and had made a huge impression on me. I couldn't understand why he was willing to leave a good, secure job with Young Life and take his wife and young family to a foreign country. When I told him that, he said something I've never forgotten. He explained, "There is a church on every corner in America, but they don't even have a written language in Peru, much less a Bible to read."

Little did I know then that one of the things that God most likes to do is to ask His people to leave what is familiar in order to follow Him. Nor did I yet have any idea how miserable you are if you try to stay in what's familiar instead of following God. Years down the road I would soon find out.

God was using all of these encounters to make me want to follow Him with all of my heart, not just a part of me. I have never liked the idea of "surrendering" to God's will. It sounds as if you are fighting God until you are too weak to fight. You *surrender* to an adversary, but you *yield* to someone you worship and love. I was tired of fighting against God's plan for me. I was ready to yield to Him.

As I neared graduation from college, my academic advisor called me one day into his office at Oklahoma University with bad news. I had transferred to OU from Spartan College of Aeronautical Engineering, a two-year training school. Mother had told me as a young boy that being an aeronautical engineer would allow me to make a career out of my fascination with planes. I began looking at magazines about aeronautical engineering and, as usual, I soon realized Mother was right. I followed her advice and never looked back.

At Spartan, the college was actually located across from an airport. We could literally watch planes landing from our dorm windows. I took every class I could with an airplane listed in the name. All of my classes there dealt with aeronautical engineering to one degree or another. I soaked it up. At Oklahoma, however, it was a different story and my grades were showing it. I had to take several courses that had little to do with an aeronautical engineering degree, much less airplanes. In fact, I was so disinterested that my advisor informed me that if I didn't get my grades up, I wasn't going to graduate!

My main weakness in school was that I read slowly. I could never be in the medical or legal profession because I can't read that quickly. The courses I had to take for aeronautical engineering didn't cover a lot of territory in books. Solving problems in calculus or chemistry doesn't require having to read 500 pages. Unfortunately, I struggled to pass courses like English, geography and history that required lots of reading.

Just as I was beginning to get a glimpse of how God could use me, my studies now threatened that future. I did not want to disappoint my parents by not being able to graduate. I especially dreaded facing Dad. He had never gone to a four-year college, having only taken some classes at Tyler Commercial College. However, he was a hard worker all of his life. He would work at the bank all day, only to come home and milk our cows in the dark. I recalled the time our cows took the opportunity to escape their fencing on the one rare occasion when it snowed in Tyler. That night Dad woke me up and made me go out in the sleeting snow to help him corral the cows and mend the fence. He taught me by example not to quit when things got tough. I hoped I wouldn't blow my dream before I'd even had a chance to get started.

After some serious dedication and creative suggestions from my advisor regarding electives I could take, I got my GPA near a 2.0 and I only needed a 1.7 to graduate. I am just glad there wasn't a lot of heavy reading involved in engineering, or I would still be in class at Oklahoma today!

Recruiters from General Dynamics (then called Convair) came to campus near graduation to interview candidates. I secured a position in Fort Worth before I got my degree. People who knew of my involvement in Young Life had always assumed I would go on staff at Young Life after college. However, I never felt called to full-time ministry. Besides, I was an airplane kind of guy. It was in my bones. I couldn't see that I would have much in common with a full-time ministry to kids. No, that wasn't in the cards for me, as far as I could tell.

After graduation I moved to Fort Worth and became a senior propulsion engineer for General Dynamics. I was now on the fast track to achieving everything I had ever wanted. But it would not be long before God would do the unimaginable and convince me to leave the one dream I'd had all my life to risk it all for Him.

CHAPTER 3

Into the Wild Blue Yonder

"I didn't know any better than to believe God."

*D*ESIGN A PLANE TO SCARE THE *R*USSIANS. Those were the basic marching orders for engineers like me. America was beginning to feel the bone-chilling winds of the Cold War blowing across our country. When I was hired as a university graduate in 1951, we were going into the Korean War and engineers were scarce. The United States was on a hiring boom in hopes of building airplanes for war in Korea.

Our company was building the massive B-36 long-range bombers. The design was not completed in time for the Korean War, but it made its debut in time to flex our muscles at the Russians. For a country kid like me, looking at plans under secret clearance for how we were going to bomb Russia was a little heady. I had already served in the Air National Guard in Oklahoma for a year and a half and was promoted to the rank of corporal. Had I not received an occupational deferment working for a company designing military aircraft, I would have likely been drafted into the service.

With only six engines, the bombers could only reach 35,000 feet, well within the range of anti-aircraft fire. My field was in the engineering section working on propulsion—how to get more bang for the buck out of these bombers. The engineers came up with a design to put four jet engines on the B-36, so that it could gain another 10,000 feet of altitude. At 45,000 feet, however, the bombers were having trouble with the spark plugs. It became my first job to trade spark plugs and see what would work best by climbing up a ladder with a mechanic and eyeballing the massive engine.

I moved into more of a design function after that, including studying the possibility of supersonic bombers—aircraft that could fly faster than Mach 1, the speed of sound. It took several years in the design phase, but the B-58 Mach 2 bomber that we came up with actually flew in 1956, the same year I got married.

Early on the engineers had solved the problem of how to fly at supersonic speed. The problem was coming up with a design that would not run out of fuel. The aircraft had to have a great enough range to get the Russians' attention. We came up with a design for a fuel pod underneath the B-58. For the first time we had a bomber available that could make it from America to Russia's shores without running out of fuel.

The first time I saw a B-58, I thought, "Oh man, this is so Buck Rogers." We actually saw the aircraft make its way down the assembly line before the public ever saw it. It could travel a long way subsonic (just under the speed of sound) at Mach 9/10ths. Then it would drop the fuel tank just in time to make a supersonic dash over the target at Mach 2—an incredible 1300 miles an hour. The best part was that this bird was so fast that the enemy never saw us. I soon figured out that the Cold War was not a technical war as much as it was an economic war. We were trying to get the Russians to spend money to defend against us. If we got a weapon, they had to get a weapon to defend against it. With the new design I helped to create, the enemy would now have to spend time figuring out how to shoot down a Mach 2 bomber.

My specific job with the B-58 was to design a cooling system for the accessories on the engine. It was not supposed to be a big airplane, but it had to hold together at twice the speed of sound. One of the tests we had to run was to see if it could fly with just three engines in case of engine failure. Tragically, the plane turned sideways in testing and fell apart, killing the whole crew. Many employees volunteered some time walking the fields of Oklahoma after the crash trying to find the telemetry tape, the equivalent of today's black box, but we never did find it.

It was very sensitive as to what we could talk about and what the public knew. I had only Secret clearance, not Top Secret, which was the highest ranked clearance level. What I was able to see firsthand blew my mind. The sign outside the conference room where we reviewed plans had a typed sign that read: "What you see and what you hear, when you leave, leave it here."

Later at the height of the Cold War, America was flying secret missions using an even more sophisticated aircraft called a U-2. It could reach altitudes above 70,000 feet, making it invulnerable to attack by Soviet anti-aircraft weapons. The U-2 was equipped with special cameras to take high-resolution photos of key military installations. An American pilot, Frances Gary Powers, was shot down and captured by the Soviets during one of these reconnaissance missions in 1960 during Eisenhower's administration, setting off a firestorm of threats from Russia to "bury" the United States.

As Powers had been flying a U-2 when it was shot down and recovered by the Russians, we began working on a Mach 3 design to take its place. General Dynamics was bidding against the "skunk works" department of Lockheed in Burbank, California, to get the contract for that plane, which became the SR-71. I supplied information to the people working on it, but I didn't know the scope of the project. That information was reserved for Top Secret.

In the mid-1960s the Defense Department requested a plane that both the Navy and Air Force could fly—taking off from a runway for the Air Force and from a carrier for the Navy. To make it feasible to fly off of a carrier, it had to have a retractable wing. This led to the basic design specifications for the F-111. The pilot swept the wings during supersonic flight (fast speed), and the wings moved out to a right angle for landing on a carrier (slow speed). I worked extensively on the design of this aircraft and remember standing on the edge of the runway at General Dynamics' Plant Four in Fort Worth for one of its test flights in 1965. As the two afterburner engines of the F-111 roared by, creating the loudest sound one can imagine, my heart swelled with pride.

That night as I was driving home, I knew with certainty I would not be part of another aircraft design the next year. Something else had captured my attention and my heart by this time. For the first time in my adult life, the pull was actually strong enough for me to consider leaving aviation forever.

———◦◦◦———

I had started volunteering in a local Fort Worth church as soon as I moved to town in 1951. It had been a while since I had been under the influence of my family's conservative approach to Christianity. However, Mother still wanted to influence my life in spiritual matters. With her youngest son leaving the relatively safe atmosphere of Oklahoma University and heading to the big city, she wanted to make sure I found a good church. Of course, that was as much for her sake as for mine!

She tapped her network of fellow believers in the Fort Worth area and found me a Presbyterian church on the south side of town. I dutifully visited one Sunday to appease her. My contact was supposed to be the youth minister there named Howie, but it turned out that this Howie had started pastoring another church several blocks away at Calvary Independent Church. So, I went down the street the next Sunday and soon started volunteering in the high school ministry at Calvary and later served as a deacon. Members from this church would eventually form McKinney Memorial Bible Church, a congregation that continues to have a major influence for Christ in Fort Worth. Howard "Howie" Hendricks would become a well-respected Dallas Theological Seminary professor.

When I wasn't tinkering with drawings and figures to determine the propulsion needs of supersonic aircraft, I was playing ball with teenagers at Sunday school fellowships and teaching them the Bible. We met in a home, since we did not yet have a church building. It was the best stress relief a young career man could find, especially since I'd developed a stomach ulcer when I was twenty-seven. Somehow leaving it all behind and volunteering in the student ministry was the ideal way for me to clear my head. Plus, I found myself really enjoying young people's company. One Sunday our small class of 12 students dropped to nine students when three became ill with polio. The next week we took our Sunday school class to Cook Children's Hospital to include those three teenagers, plus a few others whose beds we rolled down the hall so they could join us. The *Fort Worth Star Telegram* even captured the story in the newspaper. One boy recovered and entered the mission field, although he had to wear leg braces for life. Janet

Sharon in her TJC Apache Belle uniform

Webb, another who wore leg braces, also grew up to serve in Young Life. The third boy recovered as well, and I felt God deepen my love for students through this extraordinary experience.

After I had worked at General Dynamics a few years, I began dating a beautiful blonde young lady named Sharon. She was three years my junior. My roommate at OU was actually dating her first when she was a student at Southern Methodist University. When he showed me her picture in her Apache Bell uniform at Tyler Junior College before she transferred to SMU, I knew I had to wrestle her away from him one day! I moved in swiftly when their relationship cooled off. After I graduated, Sharon began teaching at Boude Story Junior High in the Oak Cliff area of Dallas, but she had an aunt in Fort Worth. She often came to visit me and stayed the weekend with her aunt while we were dating. She was a strong believer and also enjoyed serving with young people in the church like I did.

My world was coming together now. I was serving the Lord with a girl I adored. She happened to be the same Tyler girl I had visited in the hospital years ago at Star Ranch! I had a special feeling that she was "the one." I had a successful career in engineering doing something I loved. So it came as quite a surprise when I felt it was the right time to ask Sharon to marry me and she said no! I had foolishly thought I would get her to come over to my way of thinking by declaring that we needed to break up if we weren't going to marry. But that strategy backfired when she responded, "That's fine. Let's break up."

I was heartbroken. Quickly approaching my mid-twenties, I was ready to hurry up and get married. However, true to my nature, I probably rushed too soon to the finish line. Sharon, however, wanted to take a little more time to make sure I was the one for her. She is and has always been a calming presence in my life. I went home that night and cried tears on the pages of my Bible, opened to Psalm 61:1-2: "Hear my cry, O God; listen to my prayer. From the ends of the earth I call to you, I call as my heart grows faint; lead me to the rock that is higher than I." The girl I wanted to marry did not want to marry me, and I wasn't sure she would ever change her mind.

When we began talking again and seeing each other after breaking up, I set an imaginary deadline one weekend when we went to Tyler to see her mother, Roma. Either we would keep moving forward after that Sunday, or it would be the end of our relationship. At the close of the weekend, she snuggled close to me in the car while we were driving on the way back home to her place in Dallas. "I want to tell

Dr. Robert Hill officiating our wedding ceremony on October 6, 1956

you something," she said.

Man, she was beautiful when she looked at me that way. "What's that?" I said, trying to concentrate on driving, staring straight ahead at the road.

"I really do love you." I pulled over immediately, and it took all of my strength not to ask her again to marry me right there and then. Somehow I just took it in stride and we committed to pray about getting engaged soon.

When I asked her to marry me again in the spring of 1956, to my relief, she agreed. I pushed for a June wedding, but the joke in our family is that she informed me she'd already paid for a deposit on a trip of a lifetime to Europe. She promptly left for six weeks on the Queen Mary out of New York that summer! We eventually married that fall at the church where I grew up—First Presbyterian Church in Tyler. The pastor, Dr. Robert Hill, actually knew my grandfather as a young man in Scotland, so it was very special that he officiated at our wedding ceremony. Dr. Hill was ninety years old at the time.

Our breakup when we were dating was the first bump in the road I'd experienced in a long time. This kind of scare wasn't supposed to happen to someone once he or she fully committed to Christ, I mistakenly thought. *However, I have since learned that life is complicated by design. God made it that way so that we would have to trust Him completely.* This would not be the last time that God threw me an unexpected curve to get my attention and to see how I would react.

<hr />

After we married, Sharon and I helped develop the high school program at McKinney. We often had teenagers over at our home (conveniently located three houses down from the church). We were in our late twenties with a few spare hours on our hands before we started having a family.

Sometime after our first child, Jill, was born in 1958, Sharon and I went to a Campus Crusade for Christ meeting on the Holy Spirit, taught by founder Bill Bright. He challenged us to give the Holy Spirit total control of our lives. I was eager to do that, but I wasn't sure what would happen if I did. What did God want from me? I still wasn't sure, but I began praying that God would use me any way that He pleased. I have since become convinced that we cannot expect much of significance to happen without being one hundred percent available to God's plan for our lives. The evangelist D.L. Moody is quoted as saying, "The world has yet to see what God can do with a man totally consecrated to Him. By God's help, I aim to be that man." God is not the least bit interested in our being indecisive with our time and energy.

Sharon remembers my crying out for God to use me. "If there is anything in my life standing in the way of complete availability, let me know it," I asked. I claimed what the Bible says in Isaiah 30:19, "O people of Zion, who live in Jerusalem, you will weep no more. How gracious he will be when you cry for help! As soon as he hears, he will answer you." I was spiritually and emotionally spent, but that is when God began moving me in a specific direction.

These two experiences marked the time when Sharon and I began taking a handful of teens from McKinney Bible Church with us whenever we went back to Tyler. We stayed at the cabin on my family's property, which thankfully had electricity by that time! It was a homegrown type of retreat for the kids. The guys slept on the porch, while the girls slept inside. The whole group shared the single bathroom, although the girls tended to run off the guys so they could spend an inordinate amount of time in there. Sometimes the retreats would involve special guests I happened to know from church in Tyler, but most of the time Sharon and I just taught them from the Bible ourselves. We were the proud parents of two girls at that point, with the birth of our second daughter, Allison, in 1961.

One of the group's favorite activities during the weekend retreats was rabbit hunting. A few people would pile into Dad's old jeep that we kept at the property, using headlamps to search for jackrabbits that littered the open fields. I often joked with Sharon that we wouldn't have gone down to the Tyler property so much if it hadn't been for the tenacity of one boy in our group. He happened to be one of the boys who recovered from polio from our Sunday school class. He was constantly asking me when the next retreat was so he could go hunting. Ironically, the other girl stricken with polio became our helper on these trips, too.

No doubt the youth group grew so much closer to the Lord and to each other after each of these retreats. It made me glad that I'd never pursued the wild hare of an idea I'd had one time of suggesting Dad turn the property into a turkey farm. I had read somewhere in a magazine about a successful turkey farmer, and I knew Dad knew the owner of Greenberg Turkeys in Tyler. Dad just let me talk that day instead of jumping on the idea. We weren't supposed to be raising turkeys; instead, we were raising young men and women to know the Lord.

After a few years things started getting crowded in the lakeside cabin. Dad started dropping not-so-subtle hints that maybe we should start looking for other options for these retreats. One weekend in 1963, Sharon and I decided to go visit my parents in Tyler without the teenagers. I took Dad out on the lake in the boat for him to fish one afternoon, and I could tell he had something on his mind.

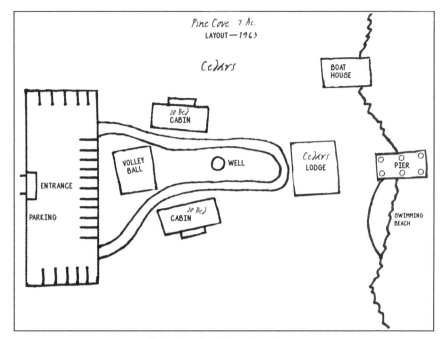

Early sketch of Pine Cove layout

"Doc," he started (we called each other Doc sometimes), "I think it's time you get out of my cabin." He dropped his line into the water and was silent after that.

I responded with the first thing that popped in my head. "Well, Doc, why don't you give me some land over here to build some other cabins and I will?" I said, nodding to the west side of the lake that formed a little cove amid soaring pine trees. To my surprise that's exactly what he agreed to do. Dad asked me to stake out seven acres for my own use, saying he would then sign the papers. Up until that moment I hadn't necessarily thought about asking Dad for some of his land for this purpose. I just knew we had outgrown the family cabin and could not continue to bring more kids on retreats unless we had more room.

Now I had seven acres in hand. I had to come up with a plan for

LIVE FOR WHAT OUTLIVES YOU

what to do with it. When we got back to our house in Fort Worth that Sunday, I took a sheet of drafting paper and began sketching a plan for three buildings. When I finished my sketch, I had a rough floor plan for a building we would call Cedars Lodge. Eventually, it would become known as the Caribou Café. It would have bedrooms, a kitchen and dining area and a large living area for meetings. Each of the other two buildings would be a 20-bed dorm, so we could host 40 people at a time. I showed the plan to Sharon, my parents and a few businessmen to get their opinions. One person pointed out that Cedars Lodge could be a Plan B for a second home on the lake if the camping idea didn't work out! However, I knew it wouldn't catch on as a camp unless we had room for 40 beds.

On paper, what I was considering doing did not make sense. I was a young father with a growing family. We didn't have extra money lying around to build something like what I envisioned. And I certainly did not have extra time in my schedule to take on something like this. However, Sharon was on board with me from the onset. As she has always done, she brought me balance. She kept me from going too fast or too far with this new idea. We've had our disagreements like any couple married for 58 years has, but we agree completely on what we believe about the Bible and ministry. We just click on the things that truly matter.

I couldn't escape my growing sense that the Lord wanted me to move forward on building a retreat where people could get away from it all and focus on God's Word in a beautiful setting. I didn't have any special ability to do that—only my availability. *I didn't know any better than to believe God.* In fact, I remember waking up each day during this part of my life and praying, "Lord, I give You my life today. I will go where You want me to go. I will do what You want me to do. I will say what You want me to say." God would soon surprise me again when He decided to take me up on that offer.

LIVE for what OutLIVES You

CHAPTER 4

Chasing a Dream

"From that day forward, we called it Pine Cove."

S HARON AND I WENT OVER TO BILL AND SUE GARRISON'S HOME
ONE NIGHT TO HAVE DINNER WITH HOWARD AND JEANNE
HENDRICKS. Bill was a Christian lawyer who served on the board
of Dallas Theological Seminary and the national boards of Young
Life and Bible Study Fellowship. He and Howard were good
friends, and I was just lucky to listen in on their conversations from
time to time. As we were talking that night, Howard mentioned
he was flying to California to speak at a Christian Education
conference at a place called Forest Home. It just so happened that
Sharon and I had planned to drive out to the same conference
the next day! I nudged Sharon under the table, signaling that I
wanted to keep this information as a surprise. I simply remarked to
Howard that the conference sounded like a wonderful idea and we
continued eating.

The following morning, Sharon and I dropped our children off
with our parents and piled into our old Ford for the 2-day journey

The future site of a showplace for God's glory!

to California. Henrietta Mears, a pioneer in Christian education on the West Coast, originally founded Forest Home in 1938. In 1937 she first visited the grounds, which were then a private resort tucked away off a winding road high in the San Bernardino Mountains. After seeing the property for the first time and realizing she could not afford it, Henrietta recalls God impressing on her heart that He wanted "His glory" to dwell in this place.[2] God miraculously provided the money to purchase the property by inspiring the son of the resort owner to sell the property that was valued at $350,000 for only $30,000 after a torrential flood had decimated the surrounding area.[3]

At Forest Home Henrietta was the first person to introduce the idea of graded camping for children and teenagers. She was also a mentor to 20th century legends in Christian education like evangelist Billy Graham and the founder of Campus Crusade for Christ, Bill Bright. We were looking forward to meeting a legend like Ms. Mears

---

[2] Forest Home website, accessed December 17, 2014. The Story of Henrietta Mears, Gospel Light, http://www.foresthome.org/aboutfh/the-forest-home-story/

[3] Ibid.

LIVE FOR WHAT **OUTLIVES** YOU

at the conference, but we assumed that we would not have a chance to do so since the conference was so big. It would also be my first opportunity to be on the grounds and see the inner-workings of a large, successful Christian camp.

As Sharon and I wound our way through the switchbacks of the San Bernardinos, the temperature gauge on our old 1961 Ford moved distinctly in the red. Just as we rolled into the parking lot of Forest Home at 5,000 feet above sea level, our radiator blew out, spewing clouds of steam. I hopped out of the car, noting that there was no one

nearby who could help us. Suddenly an older woman came over and offered a hand. It was Henrietta Mears herself! We enjoyed the weeklong conference, learning from her, Howard and other speakers. I experienced the camp with my analytical engineering mind on full power. I have always learned best by walking a property and asking lots of questions. Taking in all the information I could, I got a vision for how camping ministers to the whole family. I also began conceptualizing what we might be able to do on our property.

I felt God speak this to my heart on this very bridge

"Why don't you build a camp in Texas like Forest Home?" Howard suggested near the end of the weekend. Before I could respond, Howard added half-jokingly, "And how about building it closer to Dallas near me so I wouldn't have to travel so far?" He had a point. It would be easier for me, too, if the retreat center were closer. And most of the people who were interested in renting the facility were from the Dallas area. However, I had to focus where God was already at work—starting with seven little acres in East Texas.

The piney woods of East Texas are just magic in Dallas. The first 70 miles of Interstate 20 are pretty barren on the way to East Texas from Dallas. Then the landscape turns into rolling hills, groves of pine trees and sparkling lakes. One of the fundamental principles in developing a conference center is to move people to a different environment where they are mentally and spiritually more receptive. Two hundred acres of flat farmland two hours away wouldn't cut it for our target audience. It was important to take them to a place in contrast to where they live. What can and does take place in a conference setting, apart from the distractions of the city, is significant. Decisions made in this environment are often life-changing. It is not that people don't think about a major life decision before they are on the grounds of a camp; God simply uses the quietness of the atmosphere and the challenge of presenting God's Word in a compelling way. I was beginning to see that camping is about being in the decision-precipitating business.

When we returned home from California, I was more convinced than ever that I wanted to move on my plans to establish a camp. In addition to the original acreage our family owned, there was the potential to expand someday into the hundreds of undeveloped acres surrounding us. Since the initial purchase of 78 acres of land almost 20 years ago, Dad had been slowly adding to our property whenever land became available. He bought 110 acres to raise a few cattle. Government construction of a nearby dam had started in 1960 and was completed in 1962 to form Lake Palestine. Dad also wisely secured 25 shore-lined acres when the dam project was underway and the lake was only half-full! Even though there wasn't water yet, the potential was there for a lakeside Christian camp of some scale in East Texas. In total our family property had grown to about 200 acres, but the retreat started on just seven of those acres.

I felt I had extra time to invest in this place, but with a young family at home, money was a different matter. I did not have surplus funds to plow into the endeavor, but I was willing to risk getting a loan to give it a try. I finally went to the federal land bank and secured an $18,000 loan to build the two dorms and a multipurpose building. A contractor named Don Hill completed those three buildings in 1964, and I began renting them to other church groups when the McKinney group was not using them.

Dad would drive out to the property and unlock the gate for out-of-town guests, many of whom were in the Dallas area. He would then return on Sunday to lock everything up. I had been trying to think of a name for the fledgling retreat location for some time. One day while looking at how the cove was nestled between the pines, the name suddenly became obvious. From that day forward, we called it Pine Cove.

I continued to juggle a very demanding job, often traveling two weeks at a time all over the United States. I was now General Dynamics' senior propulsion engineer in charge of the exhaust systems of supersonic airplanes. I traveled to Hartford, Connecticut, to meet with Pratt Whitney, our engine supplier on the F-111. I also sat in on engine selection meetings at General Electric in Cincinnati, Ohio, for the B58. I kept a busy schedule, flying to Langley Field in Virginia, one of the oldest Air Force bases in the country, and Cornell University's Aeronautical Laboratory to conduct wind tunnel tests.

I hated to be gone from my family so much, either traveling or keeping long hours at the office. When I was home in Fort Worth, my mind was often divided by thoughts about the future of Pine Cove, 130 miles away. My phone was ringing a lot lately with churches and ministries on the other end of the line wanting to book a weekend at the retreat center.

In 1964, the same year the first three buildings were completed at Pine Cove, I began sniffing around for opportunities in real estate development. It was something I could do on my own schedule and still provide for my family. If I were moderately successful in real estate, then I would also be able to pursue my dreams of one day expanding Pine Cove.

My previous all-consuming ambition to work with planes brought home what Romans 12:1 says about "offering your bodies as living sacrifices, holy and pleasing to God—this is your spiritual act of worship." I would have to lay my hopes and dreams on the altar if I wanted to follow God's plan for my life. Certainly I was in a different place spiritually than I'd ever been. Just a year before, the idea of giving up my life's ambition was inconceivable. Now I had this powerful new desire to yield to a new ministry that would become Pine Cove. I had been dead-set and driven to be in aviation for so long, but I realized I would have to forego my ego in order to follow His will. One day I came across this scripture: "Delight yourself in the LORD and he will give you the desires of your heart. Commit your way to the LORD; trust in him . . . ," Psalm 37:4-5. It was strange, but my lifelong desires were suddenly changing as I grew closer to the Lord. This made it less difficult, though not easy, to make the decision to leave a job I loved.

Dad knew I was considering making a move, and he seized a golden opportunity for me one day when a local businessman came to his office. Royce Wisenbaker, who headed an engineering company in Tyler, was a hard-driving Texas A&M Aggie who had been very successful in utility development. He was also a very generous philanthropist. Dad told Mr. Wisenbaker, "My son in Fort Worth is interested in getting into real estate development. Can you give me any ideas for him?"

Mr. Wisenbaker immediately said that he had just put in the utility system in Hurst, Texas, near Dallas. He had sold it to the city and was about to do the same thing in nearby Euless. Cities thrive on utility systems, water and sewer. He told Dad to get me to connect with his broker in that area and arrange to purchase a specific 1.4 acre plot of land on a specific corner in Euless! I could not have asked for a more definitive plan than that. I put some money together and purchased the land. Since the land was later worth a lot of money, I was eventually able to build a 7-11 convenience store on the corner, along with a small shopping center. Sometime after that I built a 24-unit apartment nearby.

Thanks to the tip I had received, the projects were a success. I soon proudly informed Sharon that I had matched our income at General Dynamics where I was still working. I wasn't entirely sure that was true, but I was doing well. I took this as a positive indication of God's favor on my plans to free up more time for Pine Cove. It was my modern-day translation of Paul's tentmaking in Acts, where he made tents in order to support his gospel mission. Sharon and I then agreed that any upcoming raises I received at General Dynamics would go to fund my fledgling real estate ventures for the next couple of years. I would buy a piece of land and pay for it monthly out of the income from each raise I received at work.

Every Saturday morning after breakfast with my family, I would drive from our home in Wedgwood on the south side of Fort Worth all the way out to Euless. I never did business on Sundays. Sharon thought I was gone too much sometimes with work, real estate and travel. *But I was successful*, I reminded myself whenever I felt the pressure of all the plates I had spinning. I convinced myself that she would tolerate it. However, my supervisor at General Dynamics was not so understanding when I got in a pinch and had to make a few real estate calls at work. I was calling potential tenants for my shopping center or talking to the general contractor while trying to juggle a full workload at the office.

At the same time I had also been filling a filing cabinet at home with papers, mock-ups, notes and outlines of dreams about Pine Cove. I became a man obsessed with the idea of taking it to the next level, prayerfully seeking God's guidance at every turn. I knew the dream was there and it was worth working on, but it was not so easy to figure out the next steps.

At the beginning of 1966 I reached an impasse. Sharon helped me realize that I could not continue at this pace. I would burn out sooner than later. Something had to go. I guess I'd thought I could do it all. However, she helped me come to the conclusion that my true love was Pine Cove, and it was going to take more of my time than I could ever carve out at General Dynamics.

In recounting this story, some people always seemed a little surprised by my decision to quit my job and take this risk. "How could you do it?" they sometimes asked me. However, I felt that the question was more along the lines of how could I *not* do it? My strong family heritage in the Lord was leading me to this exact moment in my life. One could even say that I didn't seem to have much of a choice in the matter, such was the strong feeling I had of God's leading.

I sometimes wonder why more people don't make a similar about-face once they fully realize what Christ means about bidding a person to die and follow Him. I have come to the conclusion that if more people sincerely believed, as I did, what the Bible teaches about people spending eternity separated from God, they too would make drastic changes to make known the saving grace God offers through Christ. British missionary, C.T. Studd, once wrote: "Only one life, 'twill soon be past. Only what's done for Christ will last."

It was a big decision to plan to quit. It was a bigger decision to go in one day and do it. It was the first of the year in 1966, and I knew it was time to turn in my notice at General Dynamics. "If I don't do it now, I may never do it," I thought to myself. Things were going well at work, and I'd already had many opportunities that a young engineer would love to have. One of the last work responsibilities I had that year was to make a trip out to Lockheed in Burbank, California, with my supervisor to meet with Kelly Johnson, the legendary chief engineer of Lockheed and a giant in aviation design. The potential for my career was at its peak.

The day I turned in my resignation to Bob Widmer, the chief engineer of General Dynamics, was a memorable one. I'll never forget what Bob said to me as he wheeled around in his chair and looked me straight in the eye. "Mac," he said, "I have never had anyone leave a successful career in engineering and go into the real estate business."

I swallowed hard. I was thirty-six years old, hardly a time to jump ship career wise.

He continued, "I hope for your sake it's a success, but for my sake I hope it's a failure because I would like to have you back."

I wasn't so sure at that moment that I wouldn't be taking him up on his offer, hat in hand, after my first failed real estate deal. But I just shook his hand, thanked him for his time and pushed on the door leading out of his office. I was now officially unemployed, as some might have looked at it, with no one paying me a salary anymore and no one to answer to except God and myself. Dad and I were still just renting out the Pine Cove property on weekends and during the summer. The dream was still very much merely that—a dream. With my faith in God, I could only hope that I had chosen the right path.

LIVE FOR WHAT OutLIVES You

CHAPTER 5

The Right Place at the Right Time

*"The dream was no longer a dream.
It was becoming reality."*

ICOULD HARDLY BELIEVE WHAT THE MAN SITTING ACROSS FROM ME AT THE TABLE WAS SAYING ONE DAY AFTER OUR BUSINESS MEETING. "Well, Bill, I think I'll do the drawings for free. How's that?" he said matter-of-factly.

The man was Harold Prinz, a very experienced and successful architect I had now worked with for a number of months on a shopping center project of my dad's in Tyler. At this point I had quit my job and Pine Cove was on my mind anytime that real estate wasn't. I would talk with anyone who would listen about what I sensed God wanted to do with Pine Cove, including Harold. He and I were working on expanding a large shopping center on Front Street and Beckham in Tyler. Once we covered all our business items of the day, we usually talked about what was happening with Pine Cove.

I could see the vision very clearly in my head. However, I realized that most people need more concrete information in order to get behind someone's dream. If I wanted to reach more visually-oriented potential investors and supporters, I needed a master plan to demonstrate the future of Pine Cove. Once again, I found myself over my head. Drawing a viable master plan for a Christian camp was not something they had covered in engineering school! Plus, my limited experience in real estate had thus far shown me that professional site drawings were expensive.

Consequently, when Harold offered that day to develop the master plan for Pine Cove free of charge, it caught me completely by surprise. I just rested on the back of the booth speechless for a minute. *We are really going to do this*, I told myself. We finished our meeting, and I agreed to begin collecting more detailed information on what we needed at Pine Cove.

Whenever I approach a new problem or venture, I try to get as much information as I can in order to make the best decision possible. One of the first things I wanted to do after I quit my job was to determine if God was poising us to incorporate and take Pine Cove to the next level. So I set out to do my homework.

In the real estate business, if you think you have found a market for something you want to build, you do research on what people are already doing to serve that market. Harold, Dad and I eventually made a significant scouting trip out to California to revisit Forest Home and go to three other key Christian camps on the West Coast to study their operations. We visited Mount Hermon Christian Camp near Santa Cruz, California, along with Hume Lake Christian Camps in Northern California. Our final visit was to The Firs in Bellingham, Washington. These fine camps were gracious to host three curious Texans who came to them armed with a hundred questions. How did they structure their governing board? What kinds of programming worked best? How were their facilities being used?

I saw the whole picture for the first time on this trip. Beyond the programming and ministry insights I gleaned, I understood the economics of how to make camping a viable business. The camp programmed some of the time and rented their facilities some of the time, creating an income stream to keep the ministry going. We also asked for and received copies of the bylaws of governing boards and sample rental contracts from some of the camps on our West Coast tour. When we got back to our motel rooms each night, I stayed up late, studying these documents and making notes about how we might create the infrastructure of Pine Cove.

After we returned home, God then started creating a vision for four distinct areas of graded camping at Pine Cove: elementary age, junior high, senior high and family camping. In order to do this, we would need much more land to one day accommodate these distinct areas. We had a good start with a handful of acres near the lakeshore. It would one day become part of our Ranch and Timbers camps for junior high students and families. The 110 acres Dad owned eventually became the location for the Towers, designed for our youngest elementary age campers. The family cabin we owned became the camp's trail ride cabin. Yet we would still need to add much more lakeside frontage in the future to give campers plenty of opportunities to get wet and cool off in the Texas summers.

I was most excited about the idea of family camping. We had three children of our own by this time, with the birth of our son Stephen in 1966. I wanted to reach out to other families with children who did not know Christ and present the Gospel in an appealing way. While the conferences we could host for adults and other churches would be speaker-centered, I was drawn to the decentralized, counselor-centered programming for kids that I had seen was so successful at other camps on the West Coast where the staff was, in essence, the programming.

It was becoming clearer to me than ever before that Pine Cove was not about one man or one family. It was not and never has been just about Dad, me or the McKenzies. From the beginning Pine

Howard Hendricks, Bill Garrison, another friend and I praying for Pine Cove's future

Cove has been about assembling a team of believers who could rally behind what God wanted to do through this ministry. Some contributed their fervent prayers, some their finances and some, like Harold Prinz, contributed their time and talents. However, the point is that God often works in teams—at least that is what He chose to do in the story of Pine Cove's earliest days.

One of the smallest teams God used to bless Pine Cove could fit in a single boat. One day Howard Hendricks, Bill Garrison, another friend and I paddled out to the center of the lake at Pine Cove during a men's retreat for McKinney Bible Church. I wanted to show them from that lakeshore perspective how God could one day build an entire camp in those woods. We talked together and prayed, committing the land and its future into God's hands to do whatever He willed.

When Harold delivered the drawings for the Pine Cove Master Plan in early 1966, I began carrying them around in my briefcase all the time. I was ready at a moment's notice to show them to any interested party at work, in the community or at church. Harold had

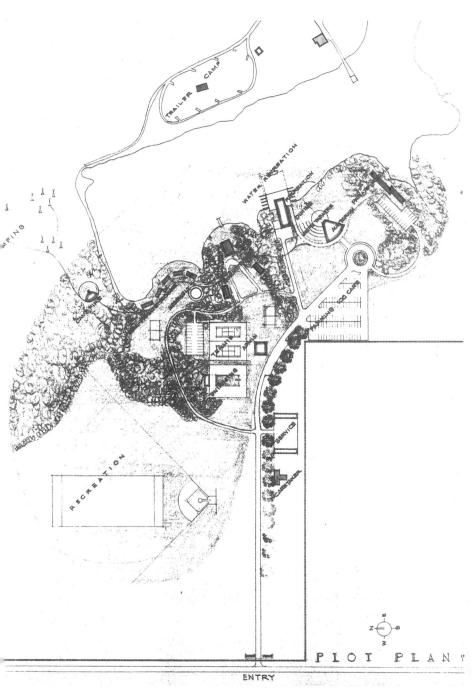

First site drawings of Pine Cove

designed a much larger two-level building with an upstairs dining room and a lower-level meeting area by the lake that could also be used for dining. He also drew what came to be known as the Azalea Lodge—a 24-room motel for guests. The drawings were of such professional quality that it looked as if we'd hired the best in the business. Indeed, God had provided the best, but he was generous enough not to charge for his work.

Nearly everyone I showed the plans to received the idea very enthusiastically, especially since many families at McKinney Bible Church in Fort Worth had already experienced a retreat at the property. However, there was a problem I kept running into whenever I mentioned the idea of Christian camping in East Texas. Anyone who has spent a summer in East Texas knows the heat and humidity can be grueling. This was a factor that the West Coast icons in camping like Forest Home did not have to consider. However, whenever anyone challenged me on it, I had the same response— air-conditioning and plenty of opportunities to get wet! If that was the biggest obstacle to this dream so far, it didn't seem like a very intimidating one to me.

True to my engineering training, I continued breaking down the process of forming a camp into a series of logical steps. I have always believed in the axiom that "where there is a will, there is a way." For any problem I faced, I always took action even if I had to change direction several times. The key to success is not giving up even when it seems impossible. You can usually come up with the right solution if you keep working at it, even after a series of failures.

For example, much later, when my daughter Allison was a teenager, she asked if I could fly her to Super Bowl 12 in New Orleans if the Cowboys played. Given her age, I wasn't sure how many more times she was going to ask for opportunities to go on a trip with her dad, so I agreed. I thought it was a pretty slim chance that the 'Boys would get to the Super Bowl. However, they did and she spent every day after school looking for tickets. On the Monday before the big game, she found two tickets, and I started researching the protocol for flying to the Super Bowl in a private plane.

The FAA put out a detailed bulletin on flying to the Super Bowl with the first item in large letters: "Do not plan to land at an airport unless you have tie down reservations." At this late date, despite my many phone calls to nearby airports, I could not find any spaces. But as a father on mission, I was undeterred. I finally found a little grass strip across the river used by an offshore drilling company that agreed to let me land there. After the Cowboys defeated the Broncos in the Superdome, we got a taxi back to the primitive airstrip. It was pitch black by now and I asked, "Where are the runway lights?" Turns out, there weren't any!

"We have smug pots that we can light and use to line the runway," the men who were there working late offered.

"Well, let's get them out," I said, noting a hangar at the end of the runway. "And open that hangar door, please, and turn on the lights," I added.

I taxied to the opposite end of the airstrip and set full power straight at the hangar. After about 1200 feet, I lifted off and easily cleared the hangar. There were so many planes coming out of New Orleans Lakefront Airport trying to access the Dallas weather report on the radio that I couldn't get a word in edgewise. When I finally did get to check weather, the ceiling in Dallas was only 300 feet and light rain. I was flying VFR (Visual Flight Rules), which meant that I couldn't fly in weather where I couldn't see the ground, and 300 feet was much too low for me to fly safely. Nearby Tyler and even Shreveport were not much better. To make matters worse, we couldn't go back to New Orleans because every hotel in every corner was sold out. About that time, I looked over and saw a 6000-foot lighted runway below in Lake Charles, a city in Calcasieu Parish, Louisiana. We landed and spent the night in a motel, proving once again that persistence pays.

The next step in my plan at Pine Cove was not nearly as difficult as securing Super Bowl plans in only a few days. I had to assemble a group of men who were willing to serve as the board of directors for Pine Cove. I'd already relied on a small group of personal friends who served as an informal advisory board during the earliest days. I also had other friends and acquaintances, including Haddon Robinson (professor of homiletics at Dallas Theological Seminary and later President of Denver Seminary), whose advice I sought. Everywhere I turned, I received nothing but enthusiasm and support.

Looking back, I realize it was no accident that God gave me a job in Fort Worth. It was no coincidence that Mother had directed me to seek out a church where Howard Hendricks had served. It was no coincidence that Sharon and I eventually became charter members of McKinney Bible Church. I am grateful that God placed me in the midst of an influential evangelical climate with many friends from Dallas Theological Seminary and other Bible churches throughout the Dallas/Fort Worth Metroplex who were committed to Christ. God supplied the right people in the right place at the right time to create and sustain Pine Cove.

It was hard to believe there had ever been a lonely time when the Lord and I alone believed that this plan would work. In my presentations with people, I showed them the master plan for Pine Cove and received an enthusiastic response. However, when I would press them to put down several thousand dollars toward the vision, they would not commit. People are like that sometimes—they need someone else to jump in first with their money before they will write a check. Having a vision with no capital but your own blood, sweat, tears and money behind it was a lonesome place to be.

Some of the men who were counseling me, including Bill Garrison and Howard Hendricks, would also become official members of Pine Cove's first board of directors. I made sure our board represented a cross-section of businessmen: a pastor, a lawyer and other devoted Christian men. My brother Robert and Dad also served on the board, and I served as board chairman. It was a thrilling moment for me and a great affirmation of God's divine plan when Pine Cove Conference

Center officially incorporated June 27, 1967. The dream was no longer a dream. It was becoming reality.

———————

The first order of business for the newly formed board of directors was to hire an executive director for Pine Cove. I have never had any intentions of being the CEO of Pine Cove. God had given me the skills to formulate a successful business and ministry plan for it, but it never would have worked if I had tried being the CEO, too. In many successful businesses and ministries, it's the exact opposite because the founder also runs it. For example, Bill Bright founded and ran Campus Crusade for Christ. Jim Rayburn founded and ran Young Life. However, Pine Cove took a unique path in that the founder served on the board, even as chairman, but never as the CEO. This strategy worked for Pine Cove and for me from the onset.

In praying through the idea of hiring someone to become our first executive director, I recalled the name of a man I had met at The Firs in Washington State: Don Anderson. This was before the day of email, of course, and we began corresponding by letter. I immediately recognized Don was a gifted Bible teacher. I also appreciated his educational background at Dallas Theological Seminary and his experience in camp programming at The Firs.

I soon flew back to a Christian camping conference at Asilomar Conference Grounds, a beautiful camping facility on the Monterrey Peninsula in Pacific Grove, California. Don was also in attendance, which gave us the opportunity to talk some more. After I arrived home from the conference, I wrote Don a letter to outline the philosophy of ministry I felt God was leading us to establish at Pine Cove. The letter is as follows:

April 28, 1967

Mr. Donald Anderson
The Firs
4605 Cable
Bellingham, Washington

Dear Don:

I have thought quite a bit about our discussions at Asilomar.

Your philosophy outline of objectives was primarily oriented to what I think we would want at Pine Cove under the types of programs which I have called Decentralized Counselor-Centered, that is: Junior, Junior High and Senior High.

I have tried to adapt your outline to the college and adult age and would like to know what your thoughts are on the same. I think the primary goal at the adult level should be to help the local church with leadership training. We can do this by programming for many churches to attend one conference or by helping an individual church put on their own conference. This type of conference would be divided into three areas:

1. Something designed to assist people in their own personal Christian life, with Bible study, etc.
2. Programs directed at teaching people good principles of Christian education.
3. An area I am real excited about: adult evangelism through couples conferences.

Another area which I think we might pursue is Family Camp, with an appeal to unsaved families, having a very loosely structured program designed to work with these people on a personal basis.

At the college level, I would like to have a week around Labor Day each year to prepare kids for the coming school year.

I have written adult objectives comparable to your kids objectives:

4. Get away from the pressure of city life
5. Enjoy favorite recreation such as fishing, golf, skiing, etc.
6. Time to think and evaluate
7. Good food
8. Enjoy the beauty of the outdoors

Since there are no parents, I think the camp objective for adults should be discussed as above.

I think the adult program would primarily center around the main conference area as shown on the master plan you have, with all sorts of flexibility by having one group use the present three buildings (The Cedars) and eat in the lower floor of the Dining Room, while another group sleeps in the private rooms and eats in the upstairs Dining Room, and a third group sleeps in the semi-private rooms and has their food taken to them.

Or, for conferences of 150-200, all three facilities could be scheduled.

Please let me hear from you with your ideas on the above program, as well as any additional leading you may have about the future.

If it is going to be possible to consider something this fall, I would like to propose your making a visit here in late May or early June.

In His service,
W.T. McKenzie

Amidst all of my careful planning, I diligently tried to listen to how God was leading us at every turn. Proverbs 16:1 says, "We can make our plans, but the final outcome is in God's hands." (TLB) I knew this to be true—no more so than in the summer of 1967 when I hit a crossroads. That was the day that I have described standing on the bridge at Pine Cove, pondering the important steps my family and I had already taken, and some irreversible ones that were still ahead of us. I was praying for God to clearly let me know how we should move ahead in faith.

At this point Pine Cove had incorporated. We had the Board of Directors in place. We had a master plan with a capacity of 200-500 people, including separate facilities for graded camping and adult conferences. We had also moved ahead and hired Don Anderson. He and his family were planning to move from Washington State in September and travel cross-country to the piney woods of East Texas.

Don Hill, the contractor who had built the first three Cedars buildings, had recently given me a cost estimate of $150,000 to build the dining hall and Azalea Lodge from the master plan. We might have been able to make do with the existing Cedars complex that first year. Yet I felt very strongly that it might be a false start not to go ahead with the two new buildings, given all the momentum we had gathered by that time.

Like most people I can sometimes second-guess what I feel the Lord is telling me to do. Despite all the assurances I'd had through others and my own personal prayers, I desperately wanted to hear a definitive answer from God. Standing on the bridge that day, I took a slow look around at this beautiful place that had been my family's sanctuary for over two decades.

That's the moment a quiet voice suddenly spoke these words to my heart: "I am going to bless this land with a showplace for My glory." It was God speaking to me—I was certain of it now—and I took that as marching orders. I left the bridge and returned to my car. I had two important appointments in Dallas to make.

CHAPTER 6

Summer of 1968

"We all had to just trust the Lord for the next day."

AFTER THAT VIVID DAY ON THE BRIDGE, I IMMEDIATELY MADE TWO PHONE CALLS. First, I planned a trip to the Republic National Bank in Dallas to see about getting a loan for $150,000 for the new buildings. My next call was to my friend and mentor, Howard Hendricks, to see if Dad and I could come by and talk to him about what we were planning to do.

When we arrived in Dallas, we went by Howie's office. I explained that I was not only asking Dad to give our lake house and 200 acres of land to Pine Cove but also to secure a $150,000 loan that afternoon—well over a million dollars today. I had recently quit my job. The only thing I could show a bank on paper was that I had walked away from making a good living, and I'd had what might have appeared as amateur's luck in a few real estate deals. As much as I wanted to make the loan myself, Dad would have to be the one to do it.

Howie listened intently before I asked him for his opinion. I took a breath and waited for his answer. We ended up waiting a whole minute without a word. Finally, he said, "Who knows but that you have come to this position for such a time as this?" paraphrasing what Mordecai said to Esther (Esther 4:14). I had my answer.

As Dad and I left Howie's office and walked across the parking lot back to our car, my father was silent. "What are you thinking, Dad?" I asked.

"Let's go to the bank and get the money," he simply said and slipped into the passenger's seat. That was Pop—decisive and willing to follow what he believed to be God's will. I wish I could say that God has always been so specific in His instructions to me as he was in that moment. He made it so evident what we were supposed to do: Go to the bank. Get the money.

It reminds me of a time many years later when I would fly to a business meeting in Skiatook, Oklahoma, for a business deal. The weather brought a 1200-foot ceiling with a very even layer of clouds on the bottom. Once again, I flew VFR at 100 feet below the cloud deck and stayed level at this altitude until I called Sheppard Air Force

Bond agreement to pay off loan

Base approach at Wichita Falls for flight following, which meant they would have me on their radar. With some surprise in his voice, the controller said, "Are you VFR?"

I quickly checked my altimeter's reading and radioed back, "Yes. I should be okay at my current altitude."

He quickly responded, "Well, sir, what you may not realize is the ground has come up underneath you. Your 1200-foot ceiling is now just 800 feet." I knew immediately that I was too low and would have to fly into the clouds to regain a safe altitude. However, I would no longer be able to see the ground if I did that. That required IFR (Instrument Flight Rules) and I was not certified to fly reading only by my instruments.

He continued, "You need to either file IFR or land as soon as possible."

"Uh oh," I thought. "Point me to an airport and I will land."

Rather than giving me a compass heading, as most controllers would do, he said, "Do you see the divided highway beneath you?"

"Yes," I responded, peering over my shoulder.

"Follow it until you see the Texaco station. Turn right, two miles to the airport."

Pilots especially get a kick out of that story, but I promise that's exactly what transpired. I did as he instructed and landed, thanking God I was out of trouble. The controller made the instructions so simple and clear because I was in immediate need of a solution. However, God doesn't always make it so easy for us. Instead of specifics, He most often gives just enough information so we will go forward in faith and trust Him for the next step. Truth be told, we prefer the times when He steps in and tells us to "turn at the Texaco" and we'll be okay. But that's not how God always works.

When Dad and I arrived at the bank, we knew Mother was back home praying for us, which gave me confidence as I walked inside. We met with the loan officer, who was an older gentleman and a little hardnosed, although he and Dad knew each other. When Dad was ready to sign the papers, the loan officer said sternly, "If the camp doesn't pay back this money, Alex, you will."

Pen in hand, Dad confidently replied, "Camp'll pay it back." He signed his name.

Once we held our first camp in the summer of 1968, supporters were eager to participate in a bond program we set up to pay off the loan. We actually ended up spending a total of $225,000 to include a home for the executive director. Those who were on site that summer saw firsthand how God was ministering to all kinds of families through

Pine Cove and they wanted to get behind it. I learned very quickly that you have to bless people before you ask them to give. The people who wanted to see Pine Cove move ahead bought the bonds. (These were mostly older people with money to invest, and they made about seven-percent interest on their investment.) At the same time younger couples made monthly contributions to Pine Cove, sacrificing some of their regular budget in order to be part of God's work.

I also wrote a letter to all of the churches, ministries and individuals who had utilized the Pine Cove property over the years. I told them what all had transpired so far and what the incorporation would mean for their future rentals. I also sent the letter to many other friends of Pine Cove who had followed with great interest what God was doing.

Dear Friends of Pine Cove Conference Center,

Pine Cove Conference Center began its present operation in May of 1964, following completion of the three existing buildings. Ownership and management have been in the hands of the McKenzie family, although broad operational policies have come from an advisory board of pastors and laymen.

The ministry of retreats, etc., on the grounds actually began as an outgrowth of the youth program of McKinney Memorial Church of Fort Worth in the late 1950s. I wish that each of you could see from our perspective how many lives have been touched through use of the grounds. This indication of the Lord's blessing has led us to further expansion. In 1966, a master plan for a conference center with a capacity of 200-500 was developed, including separate facilities for graded camping and adult conferences. During the first half of 1967, arrangements were made to establish Pine Cove Inc., a nonprofit corporation with the purpose of owning and operating camp and conference facilities: "To foster the promulgation of the great truths and principles of the Scriptures of the Old and New Testaments, inculcating them in the minds and hearts of young and old, especially by means of association and services in camps, conferences, assemblies and conventions."

Beginning September 1, 1967, Pine Cove Inc. will own and operate the present facilities on the west side of the lake under the direction of Donald E. Anderson and a corporate board of directors. Mr. Anderson comes to Pine Cove after five years as program director at the Firs Bible and Missionary Conference, Bellingham, Washington. He is a graduate of Northwestern Schools, Minneapolis, Minnesota, and Dallas Theological Seminary. We feel extremely fortunate to have a man of his caliber and experience as director.

The board desires to immediately plan to build additional housing and a dining hall. We will probably soon be able to provide food service at the present dining hall. Ultimately, Pine Cove Inc. will provide the program during the summer months and approximately half of the time during the winter, with the other half available for rental. Also Don Anderson will be available to work with any of you on planning your program.

Sincerely,
W.T. McKenzie

LIVE FOR WHAT OutLIVES You

During the rest of 1967 and early 1968, we focused on construction. In the spring of 1968, Don Hill Construction Company had almost completed the buildings, despite rain delays. At one point it rained so hard and long that some people thought we were building a swimming pool, given the giant hole in the ground for the dining hall's foundation!

In 1968 Pine Cove hosted a variety of ages during its first summer. We had a junior camp for elementary-aged kids, followed by a junior high camp the next week and a family camp the following week. The rotation would then begin again until the summer was over. Pine Cove's first summer session had 18 kids in attendance, 12 of whom were either related to Don Anderson or the McKenzie family![4] By the end of the summer about 25 summer staff members had ministered to 345 campers.

Don established the programming philosophy at Pine Cove in 1968, and we've used what he put in place ever since. First, he and I agreed that there is no distinction between sacred and secular for Christians. He often pointed to Colossians 3:11:

" . . . Christ is all and is in all," explaining that Christ is "all that a man needs and He is in all that a man does." In other words we can be as spiritual riding a horse at camp as we are sitting in a Bible study. First Corinthians 10:31 says, "So whether you eat or drink, or whatever you do, do it all for the glory of God."

Second, we wanted to practice servant leadership, which meant recruiting young college students to serve as counselors. As opposed to camps that ask churches to bring their own counselors, we wanted to train counselors as a central component of our camping philosophy. Most of the initial summer staff came from California. Don personally recruited them through his contacts on the West Coast. They spent a week in leadership training before camp started, learning our philosophy. Counselor-centered camping meant that there was no "special speaker" for kids camps. The "speaker" was the

---

[4] *40 Let's Count Em! An a(moose)ing Look at the First 40 Years of Pine Cove's Ministry*, Jenny "Special K" Lay, Pine Cove Christian Camps, 2007.

counselor who would actually be living with the kids 24-hours-a-day. They would be the ones teaching the activity classes in the morning, swimming with them in the afternoon and eating meals with them— always on display as Christ living inside them. That is the philosophy that started Pine Cove. Today it is officially called The Pine Cove Way, and we use it to train all of our staff every year.

Throughout his tenure Don also brought in influential speakers to Pine Cove for family camp where we needed a more structured program. Our first few summer speakers included names like the evangelist Luis Palau and Bible teacher Ray Stedman. One other

Caribou Café

thing Don "Coach" Anderson brought with him that first summer was the use of camp names for the counselors and staff—a tradition that has continued ever since.

That first summer we also saw how the dining hall became a natural stage for more programming, not just a place to consume meals. All the dining halls we've built throughout Pine Cove over the years have a prominent stage and a place to program through skits and announcements. The idea is to entertain and minister to campers while they are eating since we have a captive audience! A practical part of our foundational philosophy also included a commitment to quality food to go along with a high standard of excellence in our facilities so that God's message would not be hindered.

My brother Robert "Shark" McKenzie decided to visit Pine Cove that first summer, but he ended up becoming our full-time bookkeeper. We like to say that he came out for a week and ended up staying 20 years! He and Don shared a 10 x 20 portable that first

LIVE FOR WHAT OUTLIVES YOU

summer until June "June Bug" Lininger later agreed to serve as Don's administrative assistant. Kiyoshi "Tex" Kakuda was another faithful servant who was with us almost from the beginning and still serves at Pine Cove today. He tended to the landscape, planting roses and azaleas to make Pine Cove the showplace that God had said it was going to be.

Pine Cove did not make money during our first summer, but we still had to make payroll and pay our bills. The bank was taking all of my income from another apartment unit I'd built in Hurst to pay on the loan, but I figured out a workaround since I had control over the coin-operated washing and drying machines in those units. I would drive out to the apartment complex every Friday and pour all the quarters from the machines into a bag. Then I would get in my car and take the heavy bag of quarters to my brother at Pine Cove. "How much do you need this week?" I'd say as I hefted the bag onto his desk. He would then patiently roll up the quarters and take them to the bank. I imagine that no one who saw me out at the apartments unlocking the washers and dryers had any idea that I was trying to pay the bills at a Christian camp!

Rolling quarters would only get us so far, so part of our more official financial plan also dictated that we rent Pine Cove in the fall and winter every weekend. We had to rely on churches and ministries to book rentals because it was a viable way to produce income that we weren't making in the summer. Like the programming, that basic financial philosophy of year-round rentals is the same one we follow today. Pine Cove has more people on the grounds in the nine months of the school year than we have on campus in the summer.

I loved seeing all the children scampering about on the property, but I also had a special heart for families. I enjoyed seeing couples come in one way and leave as entirely different people after family camp. At the start of the week they were just loosening up from business, stress and frustration in their family life. However, something took place in a few days that transformed their hearts, and I saw it on their faces.

In 1968 one of the most important decisions we made prior to our opening summer was to put a door between the rooms in Azalea Lodge so that a counselor could be in the middle between the campers and form one cabin. It was a brilliant idea conceived during an otherwise ordinary board meeting, but it further cemented our philosophy of counselor-centered camping.

Ironically, I was out of town for the first official board meeting of Pine Cove in 1967 after it incorporated. I was on a very special trip around the world with Bob Pierce, the founder of World Vision. We went with some other Christian leaders to 13 nations and spent the majority of the time in the Far East. It was a humbling experience to see the bigger picture of what God was doing throughout the world. Years later, Sharon and I also had the opportunity to go on several other mission trips. For example, we went with Dr. Clayton Bell, pastor of Highland Park Presbyterian Church, to China to see his birthplace, and we accompanied Howard Hendricks and a Dallas Seminary group to Israel. Going on mission trips gives Christians a better perspective on the greater work God is doing outside of our their daily routine.

Because we love missions, Sharon and I had been supporting our missionary friend Jerry Elder (serving with Wycliffe Bible Translators) for many years. He once invited us to visit him in Lima, Peru, so we could see how God was at work in the Amazon jungle. There was an uprising in Lima when we were there, and the local police were trying to disperse the crowds right in front of us! I'll also never forget flying over the mountains to the jungle the next day in an unpressurized DC-3 with "oxygen masks" that were really just tubes blowing air at our faces. The airstrip at Paculpa was so primitive that the pilot had to buzz it a few times to scare the cattle off. I thought it was all exciting, but Sharon was more than a little relieved when we finally landed. When we finally made it into the Wycliffe base in the jungle, we met Grace (wife of the founder of Wycliffe, Cameron Townsend) and had dinner together in their home. A bonus excursion for me was taking a Helio plane on floats up the river to visit a Wycliffe translator in the jungle. Throughout our marriage

Unloading the Helio plane in Peruvian jungle

Sharon and I also traveled on many other mission trips together, including to Central America and Spain.

I am grateful to have also served in Dallas with Charles Ryrie and friends like Wendell Johnston, Bill Seay, Ed Yates, Charles Tandy and J.B. Featherston for 34 years at the Central American Mission (now renamed Camino Global) in Dallas, founded by theologian C.I. Scofield in 1898. I have never been called to be a missionary, but I have enjoyed supporting missions my entire life. I have heard 15,000 members of David Yonggi Cho's church in Seoul, Korea, sing "Amazing Grace," and I have visited Vietnamese hospitals to minister to wounded soldiers. Those are the kinds of images that stay with me and motivate me whenever I return home to Pine Cove to serve God even more passionately.

It was all by faith at Pine Cove during the early days, but God was blessing so regularly that there was no time to get discouraged—we all just kept going. One of the first speakers at Pine Cove said the Christian life is like driving at night. The headlights don't show the driver anything more than where the car is about to be. They can't show what is 20 miles down the road. I had my eye on the future, but I tried not to worry about what was going to happen in the next 10 years. We all had to just trust the Lord for the next day. That's exactly what I was doing one day in Dallas when one of the greatest and most unexpected business opportunities came along.

CHAPTER 7

Building for the Future

"We needed more property, so we began to pray earnestly for God to provide it."

FROM THE GALLERY OF THE 12TH HOLE AT THE COLONIAL COUNTRY CLUB IN FORT WORTH, I LOOKED UP AT THE ELECTRONIC SCOREBOARD TO CHECK THE SCORE. The great Arnold Palmer was in the lead, along with Billy Casper and Gene Littler. However, beside their scores, I was surprised to see a personal message on the board in bright yellow electronic type directed to me.

"Bill McKenzie call home," it read.

My heart in my throat, I imagined my family was in trouble. I immediately walked off the course to get in my car and start heading home. Anyone who knows me realizes that I am on my phone a lot of the time. Not surprisingly, I had access to one of the first "car phones" available at that time, although it didn't look anything like a cell phone today. It was basically an analog radio (like a CB) with a dedicated frequency that an operator would listen to and then patch the caller into the landline phone network. As I pulled out of the club, I called the operator and asked to be connected to my home.

"Sir, are you driving?" she asked. I was indeed driving—as fast as I could reasonably go without breaking the law.

"Please pull over and stop. I have a message for you," she instructed.

I did as she requested and what she told me next set my hair on end. "Your house is on fire. Please go home."

I was still about 15-20 minutes from home at the time. The rest of the drive seemed like an eternity. As I turned up the 3800 block of Wedgway Drive, I did not know what horror I might encounter. Suddenly I saw orange flames leaping from our garage as the fire department busily hauled their yellow hoses across my front yard, blasting water toward the open garage doors.

Someone ran up to my car when they saw me arrive and told me the news I wanted to hear. My family was unharmed. I turned and saw the four of them huddling together across the street. I parked and ran over to them to find out what had happened. Sharon had driven in the driveway earlier, not realizing a stream of gasoline had been leaking from the fuel pump. When she came to a stop in the garage, she opened the car door and was met with flames coming up toward her from underneath the car. Our one-and-a-half-year-old son was in the car seat next to her. Sharon very bravely ran around the right side, grabbed Stephen and deposited him with the boy next door who was standing in the yard. She then ran into the house to tell our girls, who were just six and ten years old, to run out the front door to the neighbor's house. As the smoke was rising she called the fire department and told them to please hurry!

The fire department did a great job of containing the fire in the garage. There was not even smoke damage inside our home. As soon as the fire department and the neighbors were gone, Sharon and I seized a teachable moment with our children about the value of life and the fleeting nature of "things." We sat down with all three of them in our den and thanked God for keeping all of us safe from what could have been an utter disaster.

We moved to Dallas shortly after that incident so I could be closer to the real estate deals I was heavily involved in at that time. Our move to Dallas also put me closer to the circle of influence of churches and other ministries who were supporting Pine Cove. Although Pine Cove was located in East Texas, most of the participants and supporters were in the Dallas area.

Sharon and I also began teaching young couples in their first three years of marriage at our new church in Dallas, Grace Bible Church. We used Titus chapter 2 to show how older couples are supposed to mentor younger couples in the Christian faith. In our experience, two people coming together from different backgrounds need about three years of mentoring in order to meld together as "one unit" in a Christian marriage. If older couples pour themselves into younger couples early on, before problems arise, the younger ones have a better chance of producing a lasting marriage focused on God's will.

At first we did not use any written curriculum. We would just have couples over to our home on Sunday nights to share the Scripture with them and pray with them. After several years we decided to put what we were teaching young couples in a booklet form. One day I had the opportunity to meet with Bill Bright, the founder of Campus Crusade for Christ. I showed him the curriculum we had put together. He took a quick glance at our plan and, as he was known to do, posed a direct question to me that caught me off guard.

"Bill, are you prepared to come on staff and implement this?" he asked.

I wasn't quick with an answer, so he suggested I call Dennis Rainey, head of Family Life Ministries, to discuss it. After attending a Weekend to Remember event hosted by Family Life, Dennis invited me to participate in helping Family Life develop follow-up material for couples to use after they left their weekend events. Husbands and wives needed help applying what they learned once they got home on Monday. Ultimately, Family Life designed the Couples Home Builder series that has since been published in 47 languages and sold over 2.5 million copies. That was a wonderful opportunity to be part of something like that, but God was about to bring me an opportunity to affect couples and families on a different level altogether.

———•◦•———

In late 1969 I was involved with a friend of mine named Jack Wilson in an apartment development in the mid-cities area. One day at lunch while we were discussing the never-ending hurdles of building codes and apartments, we decided there had to be something more fun to do than what we were currently doing. Jack wanted to go down to East Texas where he also had a home and find a new tract of land to develop. We set a date for the following Tuesday to visit East Texas, a trip I could easily make in my sleep at this point. Dad was now chairman of the board of several East Texas banks in Wood County, so I suggested that Jack and I go see each bank president and inquire about land opportunities.

On Tuesday afternoon, we were standing with a broker on the porch of a lovely lodge owned by an Odessa oilman, overlooking a beautiful 40-acre lake in East Texas. Everywhere we looked, we saw pine-topped hills and coastal Bermuda meadows. "This will sell in Dallas," I thought to myself. By the next Friday we had enlisted two other partners, including Dad, to buy the 4000-acre property called Holly Lake Ranch.

However, there was a problem in the meantime. The broker who had shown us the property had been so impressed with it himself that he had contracted to buy it from the owner! The broker was now willing to sell it to us for $200,000 more than the original asking price on an option to close on the property six months later. The second bump in the road came from the Sabine River Authority who had a claim to build a reservoir called Big Sandy. This meant they would be condemning all land under 380' mean sea level. That presented somewhat of a restriction on our plans for Holly Lake Ranch, but we moved forward cautiously.

We were so in love with the gorgeous view that we began selling parcels of the land while we had the six-month option to buy the property. Our contract to a lot buyer had a disclaimer that we would refund their money if for any reason we chose not to exercise the option to buy Holly Lake Ranch. Once we bought the property and were well into building roads and utilities, we hit one more delay. The government had just passed a regulation requiring all raw land sellers to make full disclosure as to what they planned to build and how they planned to pay for it. This new regulation came to be known as a HUD report (Housing and Urban Development). The paperwork simply meant it would take more time to complete the necessary reports before we could move forward. In our HUD report we had promised residents an 18-hole golf course among other nice amenities. I had built several apartments and a strip center by then, but this was my first golf course development. Walking the property prior to construction of the course, I came across stakes in the ground marked "12th Green" or "#16 tee box" in the middle of woods so thick that it was easy to get lost.

Finally, we began selling the lots full steam and, as predicted, it proved to be an extremely popular weekend destination for lake-loving Dallas residents who wanted to get away to the country. We couldn't sell lots fast enough to satisfy the demand. Still, we hit another roadblock in 1974 when President Nixon announced gas rationing due to an oil embargo in the Middle East. Motorists faced long lines at gas stations where owners might have a limited supply of gas or they might run out of gas altogether. In the height of price controls, odd-even rationing allowed vehicles with license plates with an odd number as the last digit to buy gas on odd-numbered days of the month, while other families could buy only on even-numbered days.

Our phones went silent. How could we sell lots 100 miles from Dallas if people could not even get enough gas to come and take a look? If no one came to buy, this would be the end of my career. At the lowest point, I cried out to God for help and wisdom. Over time the artificially created shortage of gasoline began to loosen up in Texas and sales picked up again. By 1976 we were selling six million

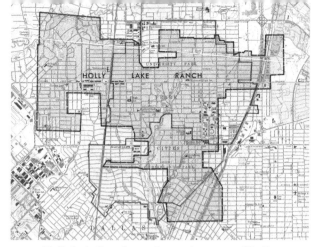

Holly Lake Ranch superimposed on map of Dallas

dollars of land per year at Holly Lake Ranch. However I did not know
how long I could ride this wave.

Cash flow was something of a challenge. It was not hard to sell
a lot for ten-percent down payment, so we made a deal with the
Dallas bank to take the note to them and borrow seventy-percent of
the ninety-percent. This worked pretty well because the bank set up
a system where they sent payment cards to the buyer and collected
payments to pay our debt. I remember at the peak, our monthly
income was $125,000. However, then the bank asked us to take some
of those notes and sell them to other banks. A genius controller who
worked for us printed out a list of zip codes, and we would then try to
find a bank in a particular zip code to go see. For example, one time
we took a package of notes to a bank when we were running in the
red and walked out on a Friday afternoon with a check for $108,000.
I drove in that night and put the money in the night deposit box. My
loan officer called me first thing Monday morning and thanked me
for the deposit. But he said I still had an overdraft!

In 1978 our debt peaked at $7,500,000, but I paid it down to
$850,000 by 1990. By then another large bank had taken over our
bank in Dallas. That's when I got a call from a young loan analyst

at the new bank one morning about my loan. I was current on every payment, but she said that the appraisal they had on our property showed that it was worth less than the loan. Since I was current on my payments, I asked what she wanted me to do. To make a long story short, I bought the note for 50 cents on the dollar! I became the bank, collected notes and went on down the road.

Pine Cove was experiencing equal success in the seventies with tremendous growth, adding more staff, campers, buildings, programming and acreage as God continued to bless us. We were able to start fleshing out our vision for graded camping with distinct camps for each age group. We built our constituency from the bottom up, moving the younger kids to the next camp as we built it. The first step in that strategy took place when Pine Cove opened the Towers for junior campers (then fourth through sixth grades) during the summer of 1971, just three years after we started. If we were going to expand further, we would need more property, so we began to pray earnestly for God to provide it.

The opportunity came when I was knee deep in developing Holly Lake Ranch and over my head as far as time involvement. Billy Hughes, a successful oilman in Tyler, talked to me about building another development in Tyler like Holly Lake Ranch. In fact, he had 200 acres of lakeshore property on Lake Palestine for sale to help get the project started. I knew my boat was full, but I told him I might be interested in the land for Pine Cove. I took a look at the property one day and I knew right away it was perfect. However, the prime location came with a steep price.

Don Anderson took several staff members on top of a hill overlooking the land and began praying that Pine Cove would one day own it and use it for ministry. When Billy heard about that, he told some friends that he didn't want to be on the wrong end of that deal, so he sold it to us! We bought the property from Billy by selling 20 waterfront lots to get enough money for a down payment.

When it was time to go to the closing on the property, I spent the prior night going over all the figures. I didn't sleep well because I realized I would have to tell Dad that by my calculations we would be about $3000 short. When I sat in his office the next day and explained the situation, at first he did not say anything. I thought I was really pushing Dad at this point because he'd already borrowed money for Pine Cove earlier.

"Well," he said, "let's just go over there to the closing and see what happens." With that, he picked up his briefcase, put on his hat and held open his office door. Dad was such an example to me of a Christian businessman who exercised tremendous faith in God. He knew as well as I did that God had provided this rare opportunity to secure the lakeshore property we needed. He would provide the means to secure it, too. Like the Israelites crossing the Jordan River at flood stage to get one step closer to the Promised Land, we just had to move forward and get our feet wet.

When we arrived at the closing, we sat down with everyone and began going over the paperwork. Dad and I looked in amazement at the final closing statement when we saw that we had received a credit for exactly $3000 dollars for taxes that we did not have to pay that day. We experienced what the Bible promises: "And my God will meet all your needs according to his glorious riches in Christ Jesus." The date we signed the papers was December 31, the last day of 1971. God was positioning Pine Cove for not only a new year but also a new level of trusting Him for all things. When we rang in the New Year later that same evening, we were celebrating and praising God for how clearly He had come through for us.

This 200-acre parcel of land eventually became the location for the Ranch and Timbers at Pine Cove. The Ranch opened in the summer of 1974 to cater to seventh through ninth graders, with almost 1200 campers in attendance during its first summer. With our programming firmly in place, Phil "Captain" Hook became Pine Cove's second executive director in 1973 and focused on developing financial stability. Pine Cove also started gaining national exposure

My Cessna Skymaster

as a premiere destination for family camp and graded camping when Phil became the president of Christian Camping International. By the late seventies Pine Cove had almost 100 summer staff members and had grown from 345 campers our first summer to over 2500.

In the eighties Pine Cove did not open any new camps, but it matured as an organization. In 1983, Dan "Yodel" Bolin became the third executive director of Pine Cove and brought his own vision for strengthening Pine Cove's ministry. He was "homegrown," having served at Pine Cove as a counselor or in leadership since 1971. Dan developed the family camps and he helped us secure even more land during his leadership.

When I look back on the early growth of Pine Cove, it seems so obvious to me that this was what God had in mind all the time. I am convinced that He would have used someone else, perhaps in some other location in the United States, to establish a Pine Cove if I had never existed. It was that important to Him. I am just grateful that I got to go along for the ride. It reminds me of the time I let my son-in-law take the controls after he had completed some flying lessons. We were on a working trip with a real estate business we had formed together. I flew us down to Austin to look at a potential deal and decided to let Doug fly us back. I told him I would handle the checklist, radio and engines. He steered us down the runway and lifted off. He did so well that I told him to make a shallow left turn and head for Dallas. Just then the departure controllers came on the radio and told us that a King Air would be passing overhead. As I saw it pass, I heard the King Air pilot radio in that a Skymaster had smoke pouring out of its rear engine. We were that Skymaster! I immediately pulled power off the rear engine, and the tower gave me the whole airport to set down the plane.

Sometimes in life God hands us the "controls" to test what we're learning in our spiritual journey, but He always has our backs. If we get into trouble, He can bring us in safely. There isn't anything to fear when we know He is always there for us. He promises: "Be strong and courageous. Do not be afraid or terrified because of them, for the LORD your God goes with you; he will never leave you nor forsake you," Deuteronomy 31:6.

After a couple of hours at a repair station, we discovered that the smoke came from a loose engine oil dipstick that was vibrating where it entered the engine case. An easy fix. I turned to Doug and said, "You are welcome to go home on Southwest Airlines, but I am going in this plane." He joined me and we made it home safely.

One of the things I love most about flying is the perspective it gives a pilot. The world looks quite different from 2500 feet. I remember flying one day over a two-lane highway. One car was following very closely behind another until it reached the top of the hill where the driver could confirm that no cars were coming and it was safe to pass. However, from my vantage point high above this scene, I knew the way was clear long before.

From a human perspective, it took a lot of faith to start Pine Cove. There were stops and starts and periods when I wanted to "wait until I knew it was safe." However, from God's perspective, He knew the way was clear all along. I did not need to hesitate. Any hesitation or doubt I felt from time to time in those earliest days of forming Pine Cove sometimes seems so foolish now. Why did I ever question what

Enjoying my love for flying

God wanted? Why wasn't I more trusting in taking those first few steps of faith?

If I'd stayed in my career as an aeronautical engineer, I'm sure I would have had a good life doing something I loved. However, God sent that lifelong dream of mine into a tailspin so He could replace it with a new one—a dream that glorified Him much more than I ever could say about my previous career.

My love affair with planes wasn't over by any means, but it had taken a back seat to my greater love for Pine Cove—and the real estate business that afforded me time to work on it. In order to keep my piloting skills sharp, I'd owned private planes from time to time. I may not have had any athletic skills to speak of, and I barely kept my head above water in school, but the one thing God did give me was the ability to fly. He even gave me opportunities to use my skills for His service from time to time through the Angel Flight program.

Angel Flight is a national organization providing free air transportation for medically related needs of individuals. As a volunteer pilot with this program, I was able to fly people who were very sick to their medical facilities in big cities. One little girl was only four years old and suffering from leukemia. She stole my heart every time she asked her mother if she could hold the controls before we took off.

I flew her several times from Nacogdoches to Dallas for her treatments. After she began to lose her hair, I told her mom one day how I had been praying for her daughter. She just gave me a warm smile and said, "I know what we want for her, but we are willing to accept whatever God has for her." I had to pull out my handkerchief and wipe tears from my eyes so I could see my controls! By God's grace this little girl made a full recovery and is now a healthy adult.

My copilot, Bill Vauter, and I also once flew a cancer patient from a small town near Holly Lake to San Antonio. I do not doubt that she will ever forget what happened that day, nor will I. We had checked and debated the weather forecast for a while before departing from Holly Lake for the trip south to San Antonio. There was an 1800-foot ceiling in Austin and a 1500-foot ceiling in San Antonio. I flew low enough to stay below the cloud deck.

As we passed over Austin, the ceiling had dropped another 300 feet in both Austin and San Antonio. Halfway between the two cities, I began talking to a controller in San Antonio. He warned me that the weather was deteriorating fast. I explained that I was flying a patient with Angel Flight and I was not comfortable turning around and going back to a higher ceiling because of the uneven, hilly terrain.

"Can you see the four-lane highway to the left?" the controller asked, eager to help me. I looked over my shoulder and confirmed I saw a gray freeway snaking along beneath me.

"Put your left wing over the freeway and just follow it," he directed. When the San Antonio airport was in sight, I lowered the gear and flaps to be in landing configuration. "You will be on a left base to runway 4," he said and ordered everyone else on the field to hold their position. I was somewhat embarrassed to see three Southwest Airlines 737s waiting in place for my little Cessna to clear the runway. After we shut down the engines on the ramp, I removed my headgear and gave my passenger an inquisitive look. Was she thinking she should just book American next time? To my relief, a smile appeared on her face as she said, "I was praying and I knew we would make it."

That's true in life. If you're praying, you know God is with you, no matter what comes your way. I would need to remember this when the ceiling soon lowered on my blue sky plans for a successful career, and some unexpected dark clouds began to gather.

LIVE FOR WHAT OutLIVES You

CHAPTER 8

A Hard Lesson to Learn

"God is not as interested in changing our circumstances as He is in seeing how we respond to the ones we already have."

MY TENTMAKING CAREER AT HOLLY LAKE RANCH LASTED THROUGHOUT TWO DECADES. No matter how busy I was with it, Pine Cove remained my priority. I recall one day overhearing my secretary say to a company employee, "He has a problem he's working on at Pine Cove, and you won't see him until that is solved." Today the Holly Lake Ranch vacation retirement community has grown to over 2000 homes, with five lakes, a community chapel and four churches. Sharon and I moved there in 1990 and our home immediately became a magnet for grandkids. They enjoyed driving the jeep and waterskiing on the lake, just 30 feet from our back door.

By the late 1990s I was still actively selling the remaining lots on the Holly Lake Ranch property. Yet I had my eye on a beautiful peninsula up on Lake Fork, a lake in East Texas known for bass fishing. I had flown over it many times. One day I decided to find out who owned it. I quickly discovered it was being held in a trust at a bank in Marshall, Texas. The next step was to go see the banker, but I was not ready to buy it so he treated me like any other tire kicker during our visit. Plus, I later found out the bank was receiving money from the estate to care for the property, so they were not necessarily in a hurry to let it go. In a few months I took the opportunity to make an offer on it. Still, the reluctant banker wasn't keen on giving me a key to the gate at the property so I could walk the land myself and study it for a potential development.

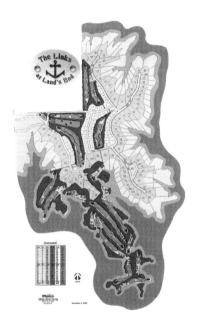

Original site map of
The Links at Land's End

When Mario Zandstra, the most recent former CEO of Pine Cove, was asked for three words to describe me, one of the words he chose was "tenacious," and I'll not disagree. I ended up driving over to the peninsula one hot summer day and hopping the fence to take a better look. I saw the stumps had all been cleared on the shore, showcasing the most incredible east-facing view I had ever seen. I struggled back to my car through the brambles, hardly noticing them tearing at my jacket. I was consumed with thoughts about a future development on this land.

When I eventually bought it, we called the peninsula Land's End after the far southwest end of England. I developed 135 lots, along with a golf course. George Williams, an architect from Abilene, figured out an ingenious way to put 13 of the holes right on the waterfront that was owned by my old nemesis, the Sabine River Authority. Fortunately, I had not burned any bridges there and with a little creative negotiating I was able to convince them to agree to let me build the golf holes on their land at a reasonable price. The Links at Land's End was born, now one of the top-rated 100 golf courses in Texas.

When Sharon and I decided to visit the real Land's End in England, we bought two anchors for the entrance of our Texas version by the same name. However, getting the pair of anchors home was another matter. We ended up paying more in shipping than we did for the anchors themselves. When they finally arrived in a Houston shipyard, Sharon and I drove down in a truck to bring them back home. The first forklift driver (who did not speak English) measured the box and my truck bed and just shook his head. Fortunately, another more creative forklift driver came along about that time. He rammed his forklift into the box until he was able to pick it up and promptly flop it into my truck bed.

When we left the port, we drove over the ship channel across a very steep bridge on I-610. As we made the incline, Sharon exclaimed, "The anchors are going to fall out, Bill!" I had to admit I felt the front tires becoming lighter on the pavement. I wondered if we wouldn't end up on our back bumper on I-610 in Houston like an upturned turtle. Fortunately, we made it home without incident. After we sold the property to Joe Munsch, CEO of Eagle Golf, Sharon and I were able to do what I had wanted to do since the first day I saw the property. God allowed us to write a check to Pine Cove that we had wanted to give for a long time. This proved once again that God gives in order for us to give back.

Throughout most of my life I had been blessed with a successful job. I also had a sense of significance from being part of a ministry that was touching so many lives. I was proud of my children and their accomplishments. *And over all this*, I told myself, *I have the Lord.* Everything seemed to be perfect, until it wasn't.

As I grew older, I was unsure of the future role I should play at Pine Cove. I feared God asking me to let go altogether. It can be difficult for founders of an organization to "find their way" as they age. The journey is long and our role takes a different shape along the way. I had to lean on the Lord to show me the right path, which He eventually did.

When I lost money in real estate developments, and believe me I've lost some over the years, I wondered if I'd lose my role as a good provider. At one time, I owed the bank 4.5 million dollars when I could not get anyone to come buy my property at Holly Lake Ranch because of the gas crisis. If I went bankrupt (which thankfully I never did), would I still be able to take care of my family in our old age? I've often said that the Lord must have known I was not able to properly handle a tremendous amount of money.

There were even times I thought I might lose Sharon—once when she wouldn't marry me and a second time when she was ill. She underwent emergency bypass surgery after her left arm began to hurt during a visit to her mother's home on Lake Palestine. We could have easily been out on the road, far from a hospital. She made a perfect recovery, but I learned that day that life is fragile indeed.

When each of these important loves of my life threatened to crumble to the ground, I realized a valuable lesson. Christ had to be the foundation of my life, not some crowning achievement or steeple at the top of a church house. He was not the cherry on top of my job, my family and my ministry. In fact, He was the "everlasting arms" underneath me, as the Word describes Him in Deuteronomy 33:27. Without God as the foundation, it didn't matter what success I built because it could all tumble down at any time.

The Bible says, "The righteous cry out, and the LORD hears them; he delivers them from all their troubles," Psalm 34:17. That is what I did, and true to His Word, God heard me. He reordered what I thought was a perfectly designed life so that He would be my foundation. Even today, whenever I am feeling down, I have to remind myself of this principle. I first mentally run through my immediate circumstances, noting where I might be able to take action to make myself feel better. I "check" my family, my business and my ministry with the Lord. It's good to stay accountable in these areas, but we sometimes convince ourselves that we'll feel better if only something in our circumstances changed. *However, I'm convinced that God is not as interested in changing our circumstances as He is in seeing how we respond to the ones we already have.*

Even though I have been walking with the Lord for many years, I am not immune to the temptation to worry or distrust my God. I am a worrier. I like to take over and solve a problem so I won't worry about it anymore. Whenever I catch myself feeling this way, I meditate on God's Word and remind myself that the Bible is true. As the old preacher has said, "Sin will keep you from God's Word, or God's Word will keep you from sin." I also keep a list of verses on index cards that focus on God's peace and I meditate on those scriptures. I remind myself that I have a big, powerful God, but am I willing to trust Him? If the answer is yes, then I cannot continue to be anxious. Finally, I start each day with a "Nothing/Everything Plan." Philippians 4:6 says, "Do not be anxious about *anything*, but in *everything*, by prayer and petition, with thanksgiving, present your requests to God." Worry about nothing; pray about everything. The result is the peace of God that "transcends all understanding" (4:7).

In 1977, I also lost Dad. However, he was so much more than that—he was my business partner, my mentor and my friend. My mother also died in 1990, bringing to a close all the prayers she had faithfully prayed for Dad and me as we worked on Pine Cove all those years. Mother was a stay-at-home mom who was always there when my brother and I came in from school. I can still remember seeing her old Scofield Reference Bible nearby on the table, thoroughly tattered and marked from use. She knew every page in there.

It became a joke around Pine Cove whenever someone had to go pull "Pop" (his camp name and the namesake of Pop McKenzie Road) out of a mud hole because he'd gotten his Cadillac sedan stuck again. Dad considered that old sedan his four-wheel drive jeep, and he often liked to get off the beaten path and drive the property in it. He had worked his way up to Senior Vice-President at the bank when he retired, and when he wasn't going off-road at Pine Cove, he was swinging badly on the golf course where I often joked that he just thought he knew how to play.

When Pop died, I was glad he had lived long enough to see that Pine Cove was going to make it. Without a doubt, he could see that it would minister to thousands of children and families for generations to come. He had successfully done what I'd only hoped I could do at that point—be part of something that would outlive him after he died.

I have had a lifelong fascination with the stories of people who were founders of organizations with far reaching influence and significant impact. I love the stories of Bill Bright and Campus Crusade for Christ and Henrietta Mears and Forest Home, in addition to businessmen like Herb Kelleher, co-founder of Southwest Airlines, and Sam Walton, founder of Wal-Mart. You're not ready to die until you have lived for something that will outlive you long after you are gone. Howard Hendricks told me when I was an ambitious young man to "look for things to do that if you don't do it, nobody else will." In other words, if there are plenty of people who can and will do something, look somewhere else to invest your life. Pursue a unique calling. I've heard many preachers say there are only two things in this world that will last for eternity—God's Word and the souls of men and women. Living for the Kingdom of God beats living for anything else that will fade away.

I didn't set out to found Pine Cove. The idea for Pine Cove came to me through divine providence and I could not help but be a part of it. Now part of me will help impact families through Christ far into the future when "Mr. Pine Cove," the nickname I earned, is just a memory. That's the way it should be and I don't mind it a bit. Even amidst the painful loss of my mother and father, I realized that life goes on without you, if you do it right.

———•◦•———

When Sharon married me, she probably didn't realize the extent to which I loved sports. When we married in 1956 we drove across West Texas on our way to New Mexico for our honeymoon. We were

Commemorating Don Larsen's game

listening to game five in the World Series between the New York Yankees and defending champions the Brooklyn Dodgers. I pulled over to the side of the road to listen to the final three outs as pitcher Don Larsen made history pitching the only perfect World Series game. When Sharon and I celebrated our 50th wedding anniversary, Allison presented me with a copy of the box score of the game signed by Don Larsen, along with a letter from him, and Stephen gave me a recording of the last three outs! During our honeymoon stay in New Mexico, we played golf at 9000 feet in Cloud Croft. I also made sure we watched the conclusion of the World Series in the lobby of the LaFonda hotel in Santa Fe. At the end of the week, I made plans for us to swing by the Texas–Oklahoma University game in Dallas for good measure.

I am obsessed with sports, but I was never good at any of them. My family likes to point out that my only hole-in-one came by way of clipping a tree limb before hitting the green and rolling into the #7 hole at Holly Lake Ranch. Although I never achieved my childhood fantasy of becoming a professional athlete, the Lord saw fit to fulfill a need I had that only He fully understood. However, He did it in unexpected ways, which seems to be the pattern God uses with me. From playing a hole of golf with Byron Nelson, to an out-of-the-blue request to pick up Tommy Lasorda at the airport, God was always surprising me. Call it the McKenzie luck if you will, but I'll tell you that my Heavenly Father was behind it as sure as He was behind everything that happened with Pine Cove.

Jerry Kindall was one such encounter. He played shortstop at the University of Minnesota and led the Big Ten in home runs, RBIs and batting averages. He signed with the Cubs and was sent to the Fort Worth Cats to learn to play second base with Ernie Banks. One day a mutual friend called me and suggested we help the Kindalls find a home in Fort Worth and get settled. This began a lifelong friendship with the Kindalls. We shared the ups and downs of life, career changes and even the death of his first wife and his remarriage to Diane Sargent, the widow of Rod Sargent—a longtime leader with The Navigators. Jerry played with the Cubs four years, the Cleveland Indians three years and later traded to the Twins where his team went on to play in the World Series. However, Jerry found his real niche as a coach at the University of Arizona where he won three College World Series. Sharon and I also attended Jerry's induction into the College Baseball Hall of Fame in Lubbock, Texas.

I loved having a close connection with a real sports hero, something I had longed for but had no ability to achieve myself. One day I ran into Jerry when his team was facing off against Stanford. We also happened to be there visiting our daughter who served on staff with Campus Crusade for Christ. Jerry had just been praying for God to show him someone to speak at a team chapel that day because his speaker was ill. At his request, I led his team in a spontaneous devotion, and we later sat right behind the Arizona dugout for the game.

Years later I took my grandsons Chris and John to meet Jerry during spring training in Tucson. Both boys were big baseball fans, and their father had promised to take each to a Major League Baseball game of their choice. Chris chose to see the Houston Astros in Wrigley Field, where he sat in the centerfield and caught a ball thrown by centerfielder Willy Taveras after he

Spending time with grandchildren, Chris and John

pulled in a fly. On our trip to Tucson, Willy happened to be playing for the Colorado Rockies who were at this spring training. After an introduction by Jerry, one of the VP's for the Rockies invited Chris to crawl through the dugout and come to the batting cage. Chris thought he'd died and gone to heaven when Willy took his turn at batting and the VP introduced them afterward. Chris timidly produced the ball that Willy had thrown him in Wrigley Field and he graciously signed it!

Another blessing arising from Jerry's friendship over the years was yet to come. One day he called me in Dallas from Arizona with a special favor to ask. He instructed me to go out to Delta Airlines gate 34 in the morning to pick up a special guest. I had my schedule clear, so I agreed to do it. Then he told me the name of his guest: Tommy Lasorda, the famous Dodgers manager. Jerry needed me to take him and his lovely wife, Jo, to the private jet area so he could zip over to Tucson for a fundraiser by noon. I asked another avid baseball friend, Bob Shoemaker, to come along with me. Driving the Lasordas to the private jet was the most amazing 20 minutes of nonstop baseball talk I'd ever experienced. As he left, he turned to me, wrote his home

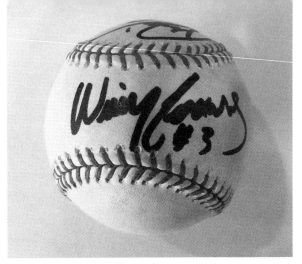

Signed by Will Taveras for my grandson, Chris

number down on a piece of paper and said, "If you ever need Dodgers tickets, call me."

Several years later we decided to make a Dodgers game the weekend our son Stephen graduated from Biola University in California. I dug out Lasorda's number and called. His wife answered and I quickly reminded her who I was, hoping she would remember her husband's offer of tickets. She gave me his private office number and told me to call him on game day, which I did. After several rings someone answered with a cool, "Hello." I introduced myself and quietly asked for Lasorda. To my delight, he came on the line and immediately asked, "Bill, how many tickets do you need?" What a day at Dodger Stadium that turned out to be!

Another time, I unexpectedly crossed paths with world-class athlete and German professional golfer, Bernhard Langer. He took a break from summer golf and came to Pine Cove with his family for family camp for several years. He gave us tickets to the Ryder Cup in Detroit when he was captain of the European team. We loved the tournament experience, although we felt out-of-place cheering for the Europeans in Detroit (especially since they soundly defeated the Americans!).

Sports have also been a way to bond with some of my grandchildren. I once took my grandson Chris to see Texas University play Nebraska for the Big Twelve title and the right to play in the national championship. Chris was a junior in high school at the time and had Texas' "burnt orange" blood flowing through his veins. Most people remember that game for Nebraska storming the field with one second on the clock before Texas kicked a winning field goal! However, I remember it because Chris told me as we walked to the car, "Pop, I will never forget this day."

The Lord was good to fulfill these desires, but He did not fulfill every desire I had, no matter how well intentioned or strong it was. For example, there were many instances when I wanted to move ahead of the Lord with Pine Cove and He held me back. I desperately wanted to add a second camp location near La Grange, Texas, as early as the eighties. I even "did the Lord a favor" and selected the land after spending a lot of time studying the Houston, San Antonio and Austin market. However, the timing was not right.

Years later, God blessed another family, the Elkins, with the inspiration to give some land in South Texas to Pine Cove, just as my family had done. Today this Pine Cove property is known as Crier Creek Family Camps. I came across an old map of South Texas in my files one day after the Elkins gave their gift. I was surprised to see that the spot I had circled years ago was very near it! The Lord wanted to expand Pine Cove, but He chose to do so in His own way and in His own perfect time.

In 1990 I presented a study to the Pine Cove board that revealed 8-9 million people were living within a two-hour drive of Pine Cove. The Dallas area was set to grow exponentially. Getting Pine Cove from 1990-2010 was going to take an enormous amount of energy, resources, planning and most of all, faith, in order to reach our potential over the next 20 years.

Along the way we tried several ideas that worked and some strategies that didn't work as well. However, there is value in giving something worthwhile a try—even when you fail. I remember when

Tommy Robinson, my roommate, who was a better player than I was, talked me into walking-on at baseball tryouts at Oklahoma University. I had only played sandlot baseball in Tyler, and I had never even been on a baseball team. The coach saw me get one hit, but I wasn't even sure how I'd done that. Somehow, we both made the first cut, but I knew I wasn't going to make it much further than that.

In the next round a pitcher during an inner squad game threw a curve ball at me. I thought, "What did that thing just do?" I just waited him out, relieved to get on base with a walk. That team went on and won the College World series that year, but they did it without me! Although I would never become an athlete, God would bless me with one more athletic encounter years later that I will never forget.

CHAPTER 9

God Can Use Anyone Willing to Serve Him

*"When you make a mistake
or even fail miserably,
do you get right back in the plane?"*

W HILE WE LIVED IN DALLAS I WAS PART OF A MEETING WITH
SOME BUSINESSMEN ON THE FIRST FRIDAY OF EVERY MONTH.
We did not have an agenda—we just met at the Dallas Country Club
for what we called "meaningful conversation"—with people like Bill
Seay, Ford Madison, Don Kerr and Tommy Jones. Some of the other
attendees included Ed Yates, Fred Smith, Lee Slaughter, Ed Drake,
Lawson Ridgeway and Cullum Thompson. Although some men have
since died and some new ones have taken their place, this group still
meets today at Park City Club.

A few of us from this group, Ford, Don, Cullum and I, also met in Fred Roach's office on Tuesday mornings to pray and share what was going on in our lives from a spiritual standpoint. We never called to confirm it—if you were in town, you were there. These two groups had an enormous impact on my life over the years.

One day a man came to our smaller Tuesday meeting and passionately pleaded with us to pray for Dallas. He was from The Fellowship in Washington D.C., sponsors of the National Prayer Breakfast. After that we went to the National Prayer Breakfast in D.C. as a group and met with other members of The Fellowship to report that we had faithfully been praying for a few years for Dallas. God then inspired Ford Madison with the idea for a Dallas Christian Leadership Prayer Breakfast. Bill Seay, the CEO of Southwestern Life and former mayor of Highland Park, enthusiastically supported the idea. We then formed a planning committee with our Tuesday group, plus Lee Slaughter, Bob Folsom (who was the mayor of Dallas at that time) and the great Hall of Fame coach, Tom Landry, who also lived in Dallas.

The inaugural Dallas Christian Leadership Prayer Breakfast met at the Anatole Hotel at 7:07am with 2000 in attendance. We heard Bobby Richardson, the New York Yankee Hall of Fame star, give one of the strongest presentations of the Gospel I have ever heard. We created quite a traffic jam that morning, prompting Mayor Folsom to remark that only in Dallas, Texas, could one create a traffic jam coming to a prayer meeting. The third year, Arkansas Athletic Director Frank Broyles was our special guest. He even came to dinner at our home the night before, along with the other committee members. I recall Frank telling Tom Landry that he had been thinking about what to say at the meeting every day for over six months! He received a standing ovation for much more than his football stories the next morning.

Once again, God delighted the little kid in me who always wanted to be around sports heroes. However, I never expected that this leadership prayer breakfast would bring Tom Landry and Frank

Broyles into my living room or put me next to Oklahoma Sooner and pro football player Representative J.C. Watts.

One year our little group had the opportunity to host a premier in Dallas for the release of Charles Colson's film based on his book, *Born Again*. "Chuck," as he preferred to be called was former Special Counsel to President Nixon and the founder of two ministries: Prison Fellowship and BreakPoint. When he called me to help arrange his visit to Dallas, I was flattered. However, I had to tell him the truth—my name wasn't strong enough to carry an event like that. Fortunately, Trammel Crow (a great Christian businessman) offered to spearhead the event and even hosted Chuck at his guest home for the night. Chuck also asked me to come to a meeting that happened to be in California with other premier coordinators from several other cities that were also hosting premiers so we could all be uniform in performing our duties.

On the day of the premier in Dallas, I drove Chuck around to radio and television interviews, and Sharon made lunch for him, his wife Patty and us. Knowing Tom Landry would be unable to attend the premier because he was getting ready for the Washington Redskins game that week, I offered to arrange for Chuck and Tom to meet briefly later in the day. I had the number for the Cowboys' office and talked to the coaches' secretary. After a long hold, she told us to come to the office and arrive at her desk at exactly 3:17 to meet with Tom during a break in his meetings.

I never let on to Chuck that I was sweating bullets to get down Central Expressway at the directed time. After arriving on time and sitting for only a moment at the secretary's office, she asked us to follow her down the hall to Coach Landry's office. I nearly fainted as I heard myself say, "Chuck Colson, this is Tom Landry." I stood to the side, listening to these two giants in the Christian faith talk. Coach Landry wanted Chuck to meet his staff, so he walked him down the hall where a meeting was in progress. Coach Landry jokingly announced, "Cover up those Washington game plans—I have a spy here."

At exactly 3:41, we were escorted back to the elevator, but the fun was not over yet. As we walked across the lobby, none other than Roger Staubach (the greatest quarterback in Cowboys history) walked in. At the end of a successful movie premier on Tuesday, I had to pinch myself to make sure all that had transpired was not a dream. Who would have thought a kid from Kerrville would be witness to such a tremendous work of God? No wonder the Bible says that God is able to do "immeasurably more than all we can ask or imagine..." (Ephesians 3:20). Many people in Dallas heard how to be born again.

———•◦•———

When my family gave 200 acres of land and the existing buildings to Pine Cove after it incorporated, it was important to us that the camp received it with no strings attached. In contrast to many camps, this land belongs to the non-profit corporation, not the founding family. It was a gift, free and clear, so that if something happened to us, things would continue on at Pine Cove without interruption by lawyers trying to straighten out who owned what.

Quite by accident, however, my family eventually received another nearby lake and 85 acres of land for our personal use. In 2007 I had shoulder surgery, followed by a few weeks of physical therapy. One day I left my business card with the physical therapist to contact me about my next series of appointments. She looked at my card, which read: Real Estate Consultant. She then looked up at me and asked, "Could you help me with some real estate?"

I assured her I'd be happy to try. I learned that she was one of four sisters who had inherited 236 acres of land when their parents had died three years earlier. The parents' wish was to divide the land equally, but the land was very diverse with meadows, hills, trees and creeks. With her permission I agreed to walk the property myself and propose a fair division of the land as I saw it. It is second nature to me to get a feel for a piece of land by walking the entire length of it. I visualize ideas very quickly when I am on a piece of property. Next I talked to each sister to see what she wanted. For example, one wanted road front access, while another wanted pasture for cattle. To get

I enjoyed the privilege of meeting Chuck Colson

something moving, I offered to pay cash for 75 acres of ditches, trees and creeks. I knew they could split the cash.

I then sat down with their lawyer who was handling the probate and drew a plan for pastures and road frontage to satisfy all four women. I ended up with 85 acres in the end with heavy woods and a perfect future lake site with two spring fed streams. In time, I built the lake and made other improvements before selling the property to my daughter Jill and her husband Doug. They built two guest cabins, a main house and a barn to recreate the setting for the family times I'd enjoyed as a child. To my great surprise and delight, Pine Cove honored us in 2014 by giving us back the multipurpose building I'd built over 50 years ago. The Caribou Café moved to its new home on our family's property in early 2015, as Pine Cove was doing renovations.

During the late 1990s Pine Cove purchased another 300 acres of lakeshore acreage. Dan Bolin led us to build the Shores and Bluffs, a prime location for our high school camp and family camps. It has a panoramic view overlooking the lake that Texans typically don't see unless they drive over to the Ozarks! In 1998 Pine Cove also transitioned to hiring its fourth CEO. I had a strong conviction that we were set for enormous growth and felt we needed a Christian with an experienced business background. The board hired a headhunter to help steer the hiring committee. So, it surprised me when Mario Zandstra, who had served on the board of Pine Cove for many years and was on the hiring committee, pulled me aside after a meeting and requested to step down. He said he wanted to be considered as an applicant for the position of President and CEO of Pine Cove. I was thrilled and could not hide the tears that came to my eyes as I said, "I had a feeling it might be you." Of course, Mario went through the candidacy process as everyone else did, but God clearly showed all of us that he was the man to lead us into the next century. When I introduced Mario to the staff as their new leader, I said, "Pine Cove is poised for enormous growth, and this is the man to lead us there."

Although Mario and I developed a close friendship over the years, one of our favorite stories to tell is about the day I almost "killed" both of us. After Pine Cove acquired Crier Creek, I would occasionally fly staff down for the day to do some work. I would always land at the nice LaGrange airport with its 6000 feet of paved runway. However, it is located about 20 miles from Crier Creek, so someone from camp always had to come get us. One day as we were driving from the airport, I noticed a small grass strip off Highway 71 near a building that housed a collection of classic Thunderbirds. There was a fairly high electric line on the west end near the highway, so I decided I would never land there. I was also careful to notice the east end had some fairly low trees, but I could always safely land facing west.

On our next trip down I stopped by the collector's store to ask him if he would mind if we landed in the field next door since it was so much closer to the camp. He agreed and even offered to take us to the camp so that we would not have to interrupt anyone's work at the camp to come pick us up. As I walked back to our car, I thanked him, complimenting him on the classic T-bird he had proudly displayed on a stand out in front of his store.

pRison fellowship

POST OFFICE BOX 40562
WASHINGTON, D.C. 20016
703-790-0110

October 4, 1978

Dear Bill:

You are a very choice Brother. I was tremendously impressed with the quiet and effective way in which you handled the Dallas Premiere. I am sure that God chose you for this very work. I have seldom been at any event that went so smoothly with every detail perfectly attended to.

There would be no way that I could improve upon what happened at the Premiere. I am positive that it will be a tremendous launching for the film in Dallas, and I shall always be grateful to you, Bill, for doing such a superb job and doing it with such a beautiful spirit.

Give my love to Sharon and my thanks for her hospitality and for sharing you with us. We are putting it now in the Lord's hands. I have perfect peace about what will happen with the film.

Dallas will be a tough act to follow. I suspect that I will be subconsciously comparing all of the other cities to it. Thanks Brother for doing such a super job. Patty joins me in sending our love.

Yours in His service,

Charles W. Colson

Mr. William McKenzie
4515 Belfort Road
Dallas, TX 75205

II Tim 4:7

CWC:nmm

"Think constantly of those in prison as if you were prisoners at their side." Hebrews 13:3 (Phillips)

My brother in the Lord

On the next trip down with three staff members, we tried the new airstrip. I drug us in over the treetops, touched down and stopped about two-thirds down the runway. I was quite proud of myself. On the next trip I carried Mario alone. Like before I circled around and set up a left downwind landing over the trees to the west. I did not pay much attention to the wind direction, but as we touched down, I realized right away we had a tailwind pushing us forward. We were really moving. As we rapidly approached the beautiful T-bird on the stand, Mario cried out, "Lord, do not let us crash!"

What happened next is the quickest answer to prayer I've ever experienced. I was using full brakes, but I decided to push on only the left brake. When I did that, the plane spun 90 degrees and began to slide sideways straight for the fence. The right wing tip stopped about 20 feet short of it, and I was able to then add power and taxi back as if nothing out of the ordinary had happened!

The car owner came rushing over, remarking about the long streak of grass that was now gone where my right tire had slid to a stop. He couldn't believe that no one was hurt, but Mario and I knew God had miraculously intervened. The fact that Mario agreed to fly with me to an Aggie game even after that day is proof of our lasting friendship!

I've made plenty of mistakes in my lifetime and I'm sure that if the Lord allows me to live another day, I'll make some more. As Pine Cove became recognized at a national level in the camping world, I learned that life is not successful Christian service. Life is a relationship with Jesus Christ, and if that is okay, nothing else matters. It took me a while to learn this lesson, but I know now that God can use even our mistakes when we are walking with Him. He will often teach us an important lesson through the experience. Or, at the very least, He will remind us that life goes by a lot easier when we learn to laugh at ourselves and not take everything so seriously.

I'll never forget the day I was piloting Bob Shoemaker and our boys to go skiing at Wolf Creek Pass in Colorado. On the way home we came across West Texas into the Dallas/Fort Worth area about nine in the evening on a Sunday night on our way to Love Field. The flight

*The Caribou Café's new home on
our family property, 2015*

controller that worked me into DFW airspace, the second largest
airport in America, instructed me to fly over DFW at 90 degrees
to the runways at 3500 feet. After I passed over DFW, I waited to
be handed over to Love Field, also a busy airport and the home of
Southwest Airlines. I waited what I considered to be a reasonable
amount of time as I continued to fly toward Love Field. I was getting
pretty close and had heard nothing so far, so I asked again if I could
talk to Love Field. The DFW controller politely told me to be patient
and he would hand me over shortly.

Finally, the controller came back on the radio and said, "21GC,
contact Love Tower 118.7." The new controller at Love Field then
told me I was clear to land on runway 31 right. I turned and saw a
beautiful row of runway lights, so I dropped my gear and set landing
configuration. By that time I was already over downtown Dallas—
only a little ways from touching down. I then heard the controller
say in a stern voice, "21GC, we cleared you to 31 *right*. You are on
31 *left*. Either land and get off the runway or go around. I have a
Southwest 737 right behind you."

Fortunately, Love Field has angled taxiways that allow for a fast exit
off of the runway. I landed and scooted off the runway as soon as I

could. After we were clear of the runway, my passengers and I just sat still and took a collective breath. The 737 came in right away and we heard the roar of reverse thrust from this giant aircraft that dwarfed us. It was another moment of silence before I was comfortable telling Ground Control we needed to taxi over again and park east of runway 31 right! I had lost my concentration because I had been impatient waiting on the controllers. I heard the communication, but I did not truly listen.

How we respond to our mistakes determines our future. I remember when I had to go back to the airfield as a teenager to resume my flying lessons after I crash-landed. I went to my instructor, tail tucked between my legs. But he didn't say a word about it. He knew I was in danger of having my fear of flying replace any confidence I had left. He just nodded toward the cockpit and said, "Get back in the plane." The story of any successful Christian leader's life is a series of triumphs and failures. However, when you make a mistake or even fail miserably, do you get right back in the plane?

Throughout Pine Cove's journey, we have learned to course correct on the fly as we seek to know God's will for the future. The story of Pine Cove's past is one of amazing grace, but it is nothing compared to the story that's yet to be written about what God will do in our future.

CHAPTER 10

The Future of Pine Cove

"God has a plan, and I've seen that plan unfold at Pine Cove time after time."

B y 2014, Pine Cove Christian Camps included nine different camps on almost 1500 combined acres in East and South Texas. We expanded to include 700 acres in Columbus, Texas, through Crier Creek Family Camp and Outback and Silverado camps. At the time of this writing, we minister to 15,000 campers from Houston, Austin and San Antonio. Also in 2014, Pine Cove secured 120 acres in South Carolina to begin a new camp. In addition, Pine Cove's traveling day camp called Camp in the City was also exploding in growth as a camp ministry for kids in partnership with local churches in Dallas, Houston, Atlanta, Nashville, Baton Rouge and many other neighborhood locations throughout the Southeast.

The Lord is using Camp in the City to effectively bridge the gap between community churches and families who do not have a church home. Someone has called it a Vacation Bible School on steroids! These children have often never heard a winsome presentation of the Gospel like the one our college staff gives. In fact, one youth minister who participated in this program as a church partner pointed to the staff as a reason for Camp in the City's impact. In one week, he explained, the Pine Cove staff intentionally pour as much one-on-one time into each camper as it would take a youth church leader an entire year to do.

As an example of the incredible work God is doing, we also served our one-millionth camper in the summer of 2011. We also believe an estimated 30,000 campers came to know Christ as Savior between 1967-2014. More than 33,000 people attend youth and family camps each year and over 35,000 attend conferences, retreats and other activities annually. More than 5300 college students have served on staff at Pine Cove from its beginning. Every year, our goal is simple: greatness. We aim to hire great, godly college kids who love Jesus, train them in a great way and expect great things.

A father at a family camp a few years ago asked me if I had any idea how much pressure the family would be under 50 years after Pine Cove started. Truthfully, I had no idea. I realized that family camps were working well on the West Coast and cultural trends often start there and work their way east. Beyond that it was the Lord, in His foreknowledge, giving insight and vision to those seeking to serve Him. God positioned Pine Cove to have an incredible impact on the consequences from the breakdown of the family before it even happened. When something like that happens, you realize it's a joy to walk by faith and not know the future.

Fifty-percent of the campers at Pine Cove today are from unchurched families. Many years ago the worst thing I had to go through was wearing a bathing top at the pool. That is nothing compared with what families go through today. I remember Mother attending a Pine Cove couples conference with me one year. The topic was parenting, and she began crying during one of the sessions. Afterward, she told me she was sorry for the mistakes she was sure she had made raising us. "Mother," I told her, "you may have made a few mistakes, but I never once doubted that you loved me and thought you were doing the very best for me."

A godly heritage like the one Dad and Mother gave me is a great gift to give your family in today's world. I want to tell young parents to stay the course. Marriage is hard work. There are temptations along the way to take a different path. However, children deserve a heritage and a blessing, and the consequences of not following through on our commitments are devastating. History reveals that entire societies and cultures break down when the family crumbles.

Growing up, I was most affected by the long talks we had as a family around the dinner table. One day when I was young, my parents called Robert and me to the dining table—they had something serious to talk to us about. They had decided to tell us how much salary Dad made—$150 a month! I owe much of my character and knowledge of what is right and wrong to the stories Dad would tell from his experience at the bank. Without mentioning names, he told us about the misrepresentations and deceptions people made in an effort to get money. Mother, the straight-as-an-arrow Bible teacher, would reinforce what the Bible taught about honesty.

Many places in Scripture admonish parents to pass on God's commands. Deuteronomy 6:6-7 says, "These commandments that I give you today are to be upon your hearts. Impress them on your children. Talk about them when you sit at home and when you walk along the road, when you lie down and when you get up."

I have heard that Nick Saban, the football coach of the University of Alabama, asks all high school recruits how many times they sit down for dinner with their family. Coach Saban is looking for stability and character development in the young player. I know from experience that it begins at home. This is why we invest so much in families at Pine Cove.

Passing on the truth of God's commands is a generational responsibility. I remember a trip Sharon and I took with Howie and Jeanne Hendricks to Branson, Missouri, near Kanakuk—also

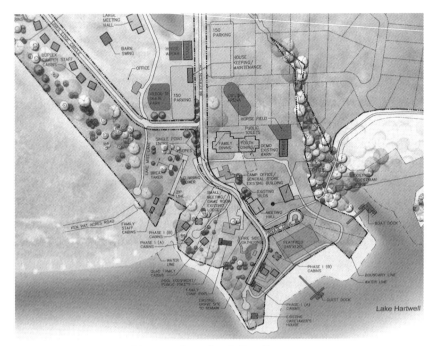

Site map of new South Carolina camp

a well-known Christian camp. I decided it would be nice to show Kanakuk to the Hendricks, so I called and left word with Executive Director Joe White's office that I would like to come visit and would be bringing Howard Hendricks. His office called back to confirm, asking, "Is this the real Howard Hendricks?" I said I did not know of others but this is a real good one!

We met with Joe the next afternoon and after a short tour, Joe asked us to join him as he dedicated a new chapel named for his father. With a small group of Kanakuk staff present, he began his speech by honoring his dad. I noticed a small baton in his hand as he talked. He then walked over to Howie and explained how his teaching had given him clarity and understanding for interpreting the Bible and had become a major part of his study process. Then, in a very emotional moment, Joe handed Howie the baton and said, "I want you to have this as a token of how you handed me the baton of understanding God's Word. "

We have a responsibility to follow through on completing whatever it is God has asked us to do. I will never forget playing golf one day prior to the annual Nelson PGA tournament at Preston Trails Golf Club in Dallas, named in honor of PGA golfer Byron Nelson. I was a member of the Salesmanship Club that sponsored the tournament, and several of us were playing with some of the media that day to drum up interest in covering the tournament. I was playing with another club member and two members of the press when Byron Nelson himself drove up to our tee and asked if he could play a hole with us! It was a long, difficult par three. We had already sprayed our shots in the general vicinity of the green, but Byron stepped up and stuck his shot four feet from the pin. After we said ooh and aah, Byron quickly added that it did not mean a thing if he didn't sink the putt. How true that is in the Christian life! I had a responsibility to "sink the putt" and keep the McKenzie's strong Christian heritage going.

Three children and nine grandchildren later, it appears they are all on a course to honor their legacy, too. Several grandchildren have had the privilege of serving in China, Latin America, Poland and Yugoslavia as short-term missionaries. Of my grandchildren, Taylor was a boat driver at Shores, Kenzie was a counselor at Timbers and Catherine was a counselor at the Ranch. Margaret was on summer staff at Timbers, Chris was a counselor at Timbers in the summer of 2015 and Ashley is still attending Pine Cove as a camper every summer. John is a past camper. My son Stephen was on resident staff as the registrar for five years after graduating from Biola University. He and his wife Rica have two young boys, Will and Matt, who will hopefully be campers one day! I believe that God let me be part of Pine Cove to help me continue the godly heritage I received. And now, by God's grace, I'm part of His work in creating another generation of truth in my family and in families across the United States.

KANAKUK MINISTRIES

*"Evangelizing and equipping the next
generation to reach the world for Christ."*

July 21, 2014

Bill -

The Article Looks great!

I've learned more about God's word from Dr. Hendricks on sixteen cassettes, than I've heard from any other teacher. Even the ones I've heard live

Dr. Hendricks' teachings are the bedrock of the Kanakuk Ministry Theology.

Grateful,

Joe White

Joe White
1353 Lake Shore Drive • Branson, MO 65616
(417) 266-3277
www.kanakuk.com

*Kanakuk Executive Director,
Joe White, a brother in the Lord*

Our mission statement today reads: "Pine Cove exists to be used by God to transform the lives of people for His purposes and His glory." There is no doubt that we use the word "transform" as it is used in Romans 12:2, in regards to being "transformed by the renewing of your mind." For some campers, this was a transformation from darkness to light (meaning salvation). Other campers were already Christians, and they experienced transformation through spiritual growth.

In fact, Mario kept a file folder full of stories of God's transformative work in campers, parents, couples and entire families through the ministry of Pine Cove.

If you read through some of those stories, as I have done, you would see God at work throughout the years. You would see families reunited after failed marriages and children witnessing their parents renew their vows publicly at family camp. You cannot put a price on a child hearing his father vow to his mother that he will never leave her as long as he is on this earth. You would also see a father praying with his daughter on a lakeside dock at sunset. You would watch as entire families choose to be baptized in a swimming pool. You might even get a lump in your own throat learning that a child lost his parent to cancer during camp but made an eternal decision to follow Christ the same week.

After a week of family camp, moms and dads return home and often begin Bible studies at work or in the neighborhood. Couples become honest with each other for the first time. Families who arrive in chaos the first day with stepdaughters barely speaking to their stepmother are the same ones huddled close by the end of the week, talking and laughing. A very distant and rebellious fifteen-year-old puts his head on his mother's shoulder during worship, and a mother will never forget it. As one parent put it in a letter, God is using Pine Cove to "plant seeds of hope" in children in ways that parents cannot.

Sharon and I have attended many conferences on marriage, parenting and family through the years. Something we meant to be a blessing to others has turned out to be an even greater blessing for us!

One of my favorite Pine Cove stories is about a young Muslim man who secretly became a Christian as a teenager. He did not tell his parents about his decision, thinking he might do so one day when he was well into his forties. He shared his testimony and was invited to apply to be a Pine Cove counselor one summer. However, the prerequisite was that he would have to reveal the truth to his parents about where he would be serving if he took the job. Fearing what they might say, he still told his parents about his conversion to Christ. Yet it was not God's timing for him to work at Pine Cove until the following summer. What a powerful testimony this young man had among our campers.

Who would have thought a Muslim man who now loves Jesus would one day serve in the Pineywoods of East Texas? God did. Who

My wonderful family at our 50th anniversary

would have imagined a young woman accompanying her friends to drop them off at camp would receive a Project 319 Pine Cove scholarship on the spot—and have to go to Wal-Mart that afternoon to buy clothes for the week? God did. These stories and thousands like them are the reason I give God praise for all He has done throughout Pine Cove.

He has a plan for every stage of a person's life, and I've seen that plan unfold at Pine Cove time after time. We give a child a basic understanding of the Gospel in the early years as a camper at Towers, Silverado, Ranch and Outback. The goal is for that camper to make a decision for Christ or confirm an earlier commitment to Him. In these early years we hope to help disciple campers in a way that will lead to growth and maturity at the junior and senior high level. Hopefully, they will return to Pine Cove as summer staff while in college. They may even be in our leadership training program, The Forge, in their later years of college or after graduation to further develop their skills. Overseas commission camping is another opportunity to expand their worldview. The end goal is to prepare campers for a life of significance serving the Lord, beginning in their early twenties and thirties.

LIVE FOR WHAT OutLIVES You

In my case I am fortunate and thankful for the years of preparation that God provided prior to the time in my thirties when He called me to step out in faith and start Pine Cove. Why delay living a life of significance in service to God until later in one's forties or fifties? I don't think Pine Cove would be near what it is today if I had continued spending the first half of my adult years building a successful career. If young people plant their feet firmly on the ground in their early years, they will have a lot more time to see God fulfilling a vision that brings glory to Him by their eighty-fourth birthday, too.

The story has long been told about Billy Graham's visit to Forest Home as a young evangelist in August of 1949.[5] By his own admission he had been struggling with doubts about his calling as an evangelist and even the authority of God's Word itself. One day at the camp he walked out into the woods, set his Bible on a wooden stump and cried out to God. He told God his reservations about the things in the Bible that he did not understand. As he fell to his knees, he committed to accept God's authoritative Word by faith.

In his own autobiography, *Just As I Am*, Graham points to that moment as the time when God empowered him in a dynamic way. The next day in his sermon at Forest Home, 400 people made a commitment to Christ.[6] Just a few weeks later, Graham would hold the historic 1949 Crusade in Los Angeles that extended to eight weeks because of the incredible response. People have since referred to the Billy Graham before and after the Los Angeles crusade. However, it is the Billy Graham before and after that night at Forest Home that made a difference. That is the powerful potential of an environment like Forest Home and Pine Cove.

I pray we'll see more of Pine Cove's influence extending far beyond Texas and South Carolina. Mario's ministry left us with a dream of the future where Pine Cove is the platform God uses to talk to

---

[5] Billy Graham Evangelistic Association, accessed January 16, 2015. http://billygraham.org/story/the-tree-stump-prayer-where-billy-graham-overcame-doubt/

[6] Ibid.

a much larger group of people about revival and what it means to confess, repent and turn to God. We can share with others what we know from 50 years of ministry, including what we've learned the hard way and what we do well. That's one of my goals in writing my story. One of our greatest opportunities in the future is to make Pine Cove available to influence the greater Kingdom of God far beyond camping so that God gets even more glory.

———◦✦◦———

Sharon and I moved to Tyler in 2007, where we still live. When we moved, it was the first time I had actually lived in the same city as Pine Cove. Forty years is a long time to drive back and forth to your dream. My family and I feel very fortunate and humbled by God for allowing us to be available in His great work through the ministry of Pine Cove. I have often likened its growth to the young lad in John 6 who gave what he had—five loaves and two fish—and the Lord mightily multiplied it. In the beginning we gave five buildings in total and 200 acres. He multiplied it through His supernatural power.

Just the other day, my daughter Jill reminded me of a time when she was a senior in high school at Highland Park in Dallas and her future husband Doug was on the football team. The team was on its way to the state finals. They were scheduled to play their archrival, Plano, on a Saturday night in Texas Stadium. The Dallas coaches looked ahead and wanted to scout the team they would play if they beat Plano. So, I flew four coaches to Houston on a Friday night after practice to scout their possible opponent. We had a big steak dinner after the game and got back to Love Field about midnight. The next night we were ahead of Plano 28-0 in the third quarter, but can you believe we lost the game 29-28! I tell this story because you can do a lot of planning and looking ahead, but you must follow through to the end if you want a victory—which is what we did at Pine Cove.

I also hope the pattern I established as a founder is a pattern other institutions of any size can follow. God gives the founder the initial burden for ministry and seeks to ensure that the concept works from both a ministry and business perspective. Then the founder steps back to serve as a board member or even as chairman but never as the CEO.

Pine Cove would never have been what it is today if I had been the CEO. It would not be what it is today if any of the executive directors in our history had remained CEO. The combination of skills and experience that Pine Cove's four executive directors brought to the table has made it successful. It is essential to have over the long haul a variety of CEOs who bring different talents. The one constant is the founder who has the responsibility to keep watch so the ministry stays on track. In my role as founder and during the first eight years as board chairman at Pine Cove, I was deeply involved in all aspects except the final decisions that only the CEO could make. In addition to avoiding the role of CEO, I also have learned another role the founder should never play. I don't believe it is possible or healthy for the founder to be the chief underwriter of the organization. In God's economy everyone needs to experience the joy of giving to His work.

Another primary reason why Pine Cove has had such a consistent story of philosophy and management from its earliest days is because of the unified, corporate wisdom of the board in the decision making process. This group of men and women are led by the Holy Spirit to share their input based on their various life experiences. I have often shared with the board my admiration for former Secretary of State Henry Kissinger's leadership and the way he conducted national security meetings. I read that he would have a strong, definite feeling about the course of action the group should take. However, he would sometimes take an opposing position and argue it in order not to overlook anything. I also like how Herb Kelleher cofounded Southwest Airlines in 1967, but he then initially relied on a CEO to execute the day-to-day operations. He was always available and involved in the big decisions, but he did not become CEO until 1981.

As the years went on, I rotated on and off the board. I even became a non-voting emeritus member of the board. However, it is difficult for the founder of any institution to know when to step aside and allow the board and staff to develop on their own. It is especially difficult when the founder acknowledges that the CEO will not only survive his or her eventual passing but also need to make decisions independent of the founder. In 2009 Pine Cove did something unique by helping me take a hard look at this idea of succession. In conjunction with some consultants who specialize in this area of generational leadership, we decided that the best future role for me was to resign as a board member.

A wonderful thing happened when I followed that advice. Although Mario resigned in 2015 as CEO after 17 years, I had the opportunity to meet with him on a one-on-one basis in a consultant role for many years, much like a father and son might do. Sharon and I pray and read the Bible together on a regular basis, something we've done throughout our marriage. Sometimes I called Mario to tell him what we read and how it was impacting our lives. We dialogued about the Christian life, ministry, parenting, marriage and many areas. We also talked about Pine Cove, but I never tried to sell my position on an issue to other board members. I felt that Mario took my perspective into consideration (although he was free to disagree with it). I always encourage older leaders who are in the twilight of their influence to invest this way in younger generations of leadership. You can take your hand off the baton and pass it forward—but still be the loudest one cheering from the sidelines.

I remember one time calling Mario to set up a personal meeting with him in town. I wanted to tell him about something God had taught me. As much as I wanted to be a mentor to him over the years, God has shown me that Mario had actually mentored me in many ways. Most of my mentors from my peer group have already gone home to heaven. As I told him these things in person at a local café, Mario began to cry tears of relief. "I thought you were going to tell me you're dying," he said, wiping his tears and smiling. We had a good laugh. I'd recently had a scare with melanoma, so he had come to the meeting prepared to hear bad news about my impending demise. "No," I assured him with a smile. "I'm still going to be around to bug you every week."

———◦•◦———

One day in 2013 when I was eighty-three years old, I received a call on behalf of the American Camping Association. They were going to host their national convention in Dallas where the Texas/Oklahoma division of camps would honor a handful of camping leaders. They called to tell me I had been nominated, along with four others, as Camp Legends. When I learned the names of the other leaders, I did a little research because I wanted to check out my "competition." I quickly discovered they were all dead! Nonetheless, at the awards banquet in Dallas I was very appreciative of the honor I received, along with my fellow posthumous honorees. I had to smile quietly, knowing I was the only one still kicking!

I don't plan on retiring anytime soon from being actively involved in a ministry I love. I am eighty-four years old at the time of this writing, and I still drive out to Pine Cove in my sedan, much like Dad did in his old Cadillac. Whenever I am there, the memories come flooding back. I'm a young man again chasing a dream. Amidst everything that is changing around me, the memories stay the same in my mind. The bar joist bridge where I first sensed God confirm His plans for Pine Cove is where they took my picture for the cover of this book. And even though my camp name is "Red Baron," I haven't sat behind the controls of an airplane in some time. However, every once in a while, I look up to see a blue sky above me and feel a deep longing to soar into that beautiful deck of white clouds. And someday—I will.

LIVE for what OutLIVES You

Afterword

I still have many things I'd like to accomplish, and writing a book was just one of them. When you're nearing the end of life's race, you think about what you want to happen at the finish line. With that in mind, I recently asked my children to write a short one-liner that they would like to share at my funeral. Since I won't be there, I wanted to know what they would say now! Here is what they shared with me:

"My dad is known by many as the founder of Pine Cove, but to Doug, our children, and me, he is known as our biggest cheerleader."
—Jill Lynn McKenzie Chesnut, 9-9-1958

"'Make your mark. Make it hard to erase.' My dad has done this."
—Allison Gayle McKenzie Maurer, 8-31-1961

"My dad has taught me many things over the years. Most of all he has taught me what it means to be a man of God. First as a Christian man, then as a husband, then as a father. Paul said, 'Imitate me as I imitate Christ.' This has been my example from Dad, and it is the example I hope to pass on to my boys. Thanks, Dad, for faithfully leading our family."
—Stephen Alexander McKenzie, 5-10-1966

LIVE for what OutLIVES You